PRAISE FOR THE AUTHOR
AND *VELCRO KISSES*

This is a story that speaks to my heart and reinforces the capacity we each have to heal from the inside out.

Susan takes us on her step-by-step journey of untangling the impact of religious and spiritual trauma that began in childhood and shaped her beliefs and choices in adulthood.

Years pass before Susan would begin the process of deconstructing everything she thought she believed—thought she knew—to reimagine and rebuild a life where she takes charge of the narrative to become the author of her own story. Courage, tenacity, resilience, and hard work have been constant companions to her reclaiming her authentic self.

This book speaks to every person that has lost a part of themselves through trauma, undue influence, unhealthy attachments, or whatever their circumstances may be.

Deep gratitude to you, Susan, for sharing your story.

—Dr. Sheree Chapell, Naturopathic Physician

This eloquent memoir, *Velcro Kisses*, is about how growing up in restrictive communities disrupted the normal development of a talented, sensitive child. Catastrophic end-time threats and religious influences created obstacles that almost cost the author her life, but the determination to develop her own identity results in a powerful sense of self-love, family, and community. This book left me thinking about ways

I might affect my children's development and thus how to maintain balanced perspectives on religion, and the world at large—particularly in these times of national and global unrest. This story is one of celebration but will also leave you thinking long after the last page is read.

—Debra, long-time friend and former business partner

When I first met Susan, I listened to her story, how she grew up from a very young age to the woman she is today. She had emerged not only from a world so strange and unfamiliar to mine, but she was flourishing, standing tall. I was in both shock and awe—shocked at how manipulation and control can have such a negative influence. I am in awe of the woman I fell for and who possessed such strength and courage to do the work necessary to start her process of positive change. I have been able to see firsthand the growth and positive transformation that my now wife has shown on her journey from living under the prophetic word, and the power that bond had over her, to seeing this independent, strong, and courageous woman who I'm so very proud of and honoured to be married to. With all my love.

—Andrew, husband and partner in life

Susan Stirling offers a raw account of how intelligent, sensitive, and dedicated individuals, driven by a deep, innate need for connection and purpose, can become deeply entangled in high-control groups and systems. Her journey spans spiritually authoritative and high-demand religious doctrines, large-group awareness trainings (LGATs), and the New Apostolic Reformation (NAR).

Stirling meticulously demonstrates the collision that occurs when a quest for meaning leads to patterned self-abandonment and an inability to recognize undue influence. She details how her resilience, talent, and pursuit of breakthrough made her vulnerable to religious childhood indoctrination and trauma bonding to prophecy.

The central metaphor of "Velcro Kisses" perfectly captures how passionate pursuits and supernatural experiences can meld one into attachments that are difficult to detach from. This book is a powerful testament to the consequences of coercive control and spiritual abuse, especially when perpetrated on children.

Her hard-won process of integration—learning to unhook herself from the pervasive influence of prophecy and creating a coherent personal narrative—is a vital roadmap for anyone seeking to recover their self trust and personal agency. This memoir illuminates why recognizing predatory behaviors is so essential, reminding us that reclaiming one's life begins with reclaiming one's story.

— **Anne L. Peterson, Author of *Is This A Cult? Confronting the Line Between Transformation and Exploitation***

Velcro Kisses

Prophecy, Trauma Bonds &
Reclaiming Narrative

SUSAN STIRLING

Velcro Kisses

Book Design | Petya Tsankova
Editor | Justin Chevrier
Publishing Management | TSPA The Self Publishing Agency, Inc.

Dedication

To all the women before me who boldly stood against structures, systems, and undue influences that tried to overpower them yet never fully reached freedom, thank you for doing what you could to make a difference. You taught me that I am far more than the sum of my experiences. As a woman, I choose to carry forward your strength and courage, building towards the freedom you dreamed of.

To all the individuals who have fought for their personal rights to be themselves despite the opposing voices, influences, and systems who told them otherwise—who broke ranks and followed their internal voice—thank you for your grit.

To Benjamin and Abigail, thank you for coming into this world. You two are my treasures in this life. You helped me keep going and you made me want to be better, know better, and live differently. You both have been my inspiration to help create a different future—one that empowers yours.

To Mariah, thank you for saying yes and joining our family. You are truly a gift. To April, Ethan, and Richard, it is my hope that you truly live your lives out loud.

To Andrew, you have embodied what it truly means to keep your word—how it looks, feels, and acts in the moments that count. Thank you for being my partner, supporting me, and encouraging me to pursue my dreams. I choose you.

And

To my younger self—I see you, I hear you, and yes, you can.

Note from the Author

My story reflects my personal experiences and perspectives. It is not written to assign blame or recount anyone else's memories, but to offer an honest account of my own journey. Writing my story has been a process of understanding, grieving, and ultimately healing, allowing me to make sense of the events that shaped my life. I have chosen to change many of the names for privacy reasons, unless permission was requested and given. Some events are recalled from memory, except in those moments where the words left an imprint or a prophecy had already been transcribed. I have described people, circumstances, and experiences as I remember them, filtered through the eyes of the age I was and the impression they left upon me. There are parts of my story that touch the lives of others, my first husband, my family of origin, and our shared beginnings. I have chosen not to unfold those details here.

Throughout the book, I have chosen to capitalize certain words that are commonly capitalized in church settings, such as *Heaven*, *Hell*, and *God's Kingdom*. I have chosen to retain this style in an effort to highlight the importance and gravity these terms had when I was in these spaces, and to help provide some familiarity to readers who might be coming out of these systems of belief. I have intentionally chosen not to capitalize titles such as *apostles* and *prophets*, although in my personal experience, these terms were capitalized in these Christian contexts and they carried the same weight as *Heaven*.

Within these pages, I tell my story of how I became trauma bonded to prophecy and how I *reclaimed* my narrative.

Hello, I'm Susan

I first began writing my story to weave together the many threads of my life. Each thread carried its own story, its own theme, its own voice. Yet, they were so tightly knotted that I could rarely follow one without bumping into another. Trying to trace an inner theme felt less like gently unraveling a blanket and more like painstakingly teasing apart a knot, thread by thread, almost as if I had to use a microneedle. The result was often a tangle of half-formed narratives and missing pieces, all circling around the same question: Why did so many of my promising beginnings veer off course and often end up going sideways?

As I became aware of just how much I had been searching for connection and belonging my whole life, the drive to fit in caused me to abandon the deepest parts of me; I broke trust with myself—the voice within me, my intuition, and my gut instinct. I learned to take the shape of whatever surrounded me. I merged my personality to fit my closest relationships. I moulded myself to fit into church communities, and I mistook structure and enmeshment for safety. The church became the backdrop of my adulthood—the place where I both belonged and slowly lost control of my story. By the time I began to unhook myself from the people and the systems I had become bonded to, I was fully immersed in the New Apostolic Reformation, where prophecy spoken through modern-day prophets directed my life. Removing myself from this system was not easy nor was it linear, and it took work—work that taught me about childhood attachment, trauma bonding, indoctrination, the sway of prophecy, large group dynamics, and ultimately, the nature of undue influence and what it takes to break free and detach one's life from it.

As a young girl, I was indoctrinated to believe that the end of the world—called the Rapture—would happen ANY DAY. Believing this changed me; waiting for the impending Rapture split my psyche, creating two "selves": my normal self and my spiritual self. My spiritual self was fueled by fear; from a quiet despair to a gnawing dread of some impending doom that always seemed just over the horizon. My ordinary, everyday self moved through a childhood that, for the most part, appeared "normal," seemingly oblivious to the undercurrent of dread shaping so much of my inner life.

In my teens and young adulthood, I experienced traumatic events that would dramatically change my life and would ultimately lead me to begin my quest seeking for answers.

In my early twenties, I entered the personal development world and attended seminars known today as large-group awareness training (LGAT) sessions. I would then return to church, where I would spend the next thirty years fully believing that I was being transformed and doing the work of the Lord, when in reality, I remained tethered to these groups and ideologies because of my deep-rooted fears, my need to belong, and my need to survive. I believed I was rebuilding my life, only to have the proverbial rug pulled out from under me again and again.

I took refuge under the banners of modern-day apostles and prophets, believing that they knew God's thoughts and mandate not only for my life but for the world. I believed that surrendering myself to their teachings would shield me from the Enemy's harm, yet it had the opposite effect. Breakthrough, spiritual warfare, prophetic intercession, and Kingdom advancement became my highest priority, exacting a cost I had yet to understand. Prophecy and the pursuit of advancing God's Kingdom on Earth became the mandate, guided by the Seven Mountain framework and its prescribed spheres of influence. I was trading my sense of self for the promise of breakthrough, belonging, and purpose.

In 2020, when I was in my fifties, the pandemic resurfaced trauma responses that had long been buried in my body and brain. In 2023, I left the clinic setting I had worked in for over a decade, and not long after, I experienced two serious physical falls that resulted in multiple surgeries. I spiraled both emotionally and physically. However, that season of falling taught me what no textbook could: how to roll. In fact, it took falling—literally and metaphorically—to see things clearly. That idea became my mantra: the art of falling.

I titled my story *Velcro Kisses*. *Velcro* came to me as I thought about what these attachments felt like and how I could describe the hold they had in my life. Hooks and loops, like Velcro, created a pattern of bonding to God, to people, and to religious groups. But it's those Kisses that melded me into these attachments. From receiving my first prophetic word and my experiences with the supernatural—Holy Spirit manifestations, learning to hear God prophetically, *rhema* words—to extended worship, receiving impartations, and prophetic dance, I had many passionate pursuits that I considered to be Kisses from Heaven. Being in the presence of God's elect, those who had received God's mandate, created a sense of mysticism that was magnetic. These Kisses sent my heart racing and energy surging through my entire body, as if igniting a fire that words could never quite describe. These experiences captivated my heart and mind beyond the physical realm.

Slowly, and with support, I began to unhook myself from those Velcro Kiss moments in my life. And as I did this work, I began to reconnect with myself, reframe my story, and rise again. Today, I walk alongside others who are untangling their own complex histories—especially those navigating patterned self-abandonment, undue influence, or spiritual and religious trauma. With a trauma-sensitive lens, as well as being a certified coach based in the neuroscience of human development, I help others discover the power of small steps, safe connections, and living from the inside out. Healing is possible in every season of life. Let's get started. Let me begin with my story.

Introduction
Learning to Pause

There we were in Costco. It was spring of 2020, and I'm struggling to maintain my composure. My chest is pounding, I can't keep my equilibrium, I feel like I'm about to throw up. I grab onto Andrew's arm to try to steady myself, trying to ascertain what the hell is happening to me. We stop. Time passes. What were likely minutes register in my mind as an eternity. My eyes glance up only to see a white cloud in a buggy pass—yes, you guessed it—toilet paper! "Oh God," I say out loud as my head swirls. *Will there be any toilet paper left by the time we get over to it?* I struggle to catch my breath, my chest is tight. *Am I in Afib again? Why can't I breathe? Oh God, I think I'm going to pass out.* "Andrew, I need to get out of here," I say as I try to steady myself. "What? We just got here?" Andrew says, and as he looks at me, our eyes lock, his face flickers—concern tangled with confusion. It's the first time Andrew has experienced this side of me. Andrew puts his hand around my waist and pulls me to him, telling me, "Susan, you're okay." But I know I'm not okay, I feel as though I'm losing all the equilibrium I've built over the last ten years.

The most shocking part about this triggering episode was that it showed that despite all the work I had done to recover from my years of indoctrination and trauma bonds to prophecy, I still had a lot of work ahead of me. On that journey, I learned the words that gave me the language and perspective I needed to understand the magnitude of the indoctrination I received as a child that was still alive in my mind and body. I may have left the church ten years ago, but the church was still very much alive in me. It was here, in this dark season, that I chose to go deep and uncover the depths of my pain and grief as it presented much more than broken bones or a broken heart.

It was through this season that I began to take up my love of writing and began to create what I heard Daniel Shaw share about having a "coherent narrative." Daniel Shaw is a psychoanalytically oriented trauma-informed psychotherapist. What he said struck a chord that resonated with me; although I didn't fully understand what it meant, I felt it to my core. In therapy, a coherent narrative comes from the process of making sense of experiences, integrating memories, and connecting emotions to events. A coherent narrative in therapy is the result of memory integration, emotional processing, meaning-making, perspective-taking, and verbal expression. It's both a psychological and neurological process; the brain literally rewires itself to hold a story rather than fragments. Through creating a coherent narrative of my experiences, I began to truly experience healing. It was here that I discovered just how strong my attachment to prophecy was—to me, it was a trauma bond that impacted many of my life choices. Choices that were unduly influenced.

I did a lot of personal work when I left the church around 2010—I returned to Canada, I began to see "secular" counsellors, I finally gave myself permission to leave my first marriage after twenty-six years, and I was no longer overinvesting and doing the heavy emotional work to keep every relationship intact. I had given myself permission to let go of any relationship that was not reciprocal. I was working at a health clinic and earning an income within an environment that aligned with my values. I had a small business on the side. I began to build new beliefs around life, self, and empowerment. I spent thousands of dollars investing in my mental, emotional, and physical health. I met Andrew, we were newly engaged. Now this! I was shell-shocked. *How could this be happening? Especially now.*

Despite building a new life in Canada over the last ten years, this breakdown in Costco told me that I still held on to something familiar—that sinking feeling that tells me I won't get my chance, that life is over before it has a chance to start. Fact was, my life was over, and I had to deconstruct it. It was time for me to begin to dismantle the story of my life.

The storyline I was living was repeating—it was an old story from many years ago, and it would seem that no matter what I did or how far I had gone, I was being triggered by something I thought was in my past, yet it was clearly still alive in me. How I dreaded the feeling of the proverbial rug being pulled out from underneath my feet again. All I could feel was the mounting anger, confusion, and despair of a conflicted belief system as the shame spiral began.

Except, this time, I paused.

And as I did, I remembered. I've lived longer this time. I'm no longer four or five years old—I'm fifty-four. It's time to double back before I move forward. And this time, as I do the work, I'll learn the art of falling, the power of embracing integration, and how to use momentum to regain my balance—this time with superpowers!

Mum's the Word

I wouldn't be here without my mother. I wrote in my mum's eulogy that she would be remembered as a gatherer. Mum had the ability to gather many people together. Family, food, and fellowship were high on my mother's list for living a good life. Family meals would come to outgrow our family's kitchen table; we would add table extensions, then another table, and still there were always more to feed. So, of course, it was the natural thing to rent the Moose Hall in our hamlet so that friends, who were as family, could share meals. Special occasions were just that: special. I recall as a young girl, my mum would often sew special outfits and skate costumes, as well as baking special birthday cakes of my choosing in my early years. It was common to find Mum busy: from being active in the community, to supporting my sports events, to eventually being elected as a town council representative. Mum showed me that a woman could make a difference in family, in friendship, and in life.

Being the youngest gave me the opportunity and the role of becoming my mum's companion as she began her born-again experience. Mum's born-again experience, as far as I know, began in the 1970s when the Jesus People Movement was giving way to the evangelical movement. The Jesus People Movement left a powerful legacy, including the formation of many new Christian organizations, denominations, church groups, and its influence in the development of the Christian right and the Christian left. The charismatic movement testified to having supernatural experiences like those recorded in the book of Acts, especially speaking in tongues. These two movements, the charismatic movement and the Jesus Movement, believed they were calling the Church back to a more biblically accurate version of Christianity and that these changes would result in the restoration of the spiritual gifts in the Church. Expo '72 had over 80,000 Jesus People attending; however, by the late 1980s, the movement began to subside but not without leaving a major influence in Christian music, youth, and church life. Parachurch organizations and Pentecostal churches formed under this charismatic movement, where spiritual manifestation of the gifts of the Holy Spirit were not uncommon.

House churches were also part of this movement, and this is where I first remember *church*. I never fully learned the specific vulnerabilities that led to my mum's conversion to Christianity. What I can recall is that we spent a summer in the Yukon visiting my aunt. My aunt and her husband had house meetings, and they also had an outhouse with an owl that lived in the tree nearby that would scare the heebie-jeebies out of me each time I had to pee at night. That summer, my mum "got saved." And when we came up the escalator at the Calgary International Airport to meet my dad, as they embraced, I remember feeling anxious about the change my mum went through that my dad was completely unaware of. From that time to the time of my mum's departure from this world, it was clear that my mum's search for spiritual significance and spiritual purpose would be irreversibly shaped by her experience that summer.

Through the many phases of my mum's life, one thing that remained constant was her belief that Jesus would return and that those with eyes to see and ears to hear would see and understand the signs of the times. As an adult woman with a family of my own, Mum would still try to hand me the latest book about the most recent prophetic revelation or sign in the night sky that confirmed that the end times were at hand. Yet, at the same time, my mum would be the person who would show me in her forties that she could re-enter the workforce; in her fifties, she could be elected and bring change to her surrounding community for not one term, but two; in her sixties, she showed me that she still had what it took to gather the courage needed to create change in her life and divorce and rebuild her life. Then, still not defined by age at seventy, I would watch as Mum remarried and found happiness.

COVID took much from many people. It was during the pandemic in 2021 that dementia would ultimately take my mum, and it was during COVID that I would begin to feel the impact of just how much my spiritual life had taken from me. I would embrace Mum for the last time behind the locked doors of extended care at the hospital in the same town Mum spent most of her life, and as I did, I could feel myself travelling back in time trying to recapture all the things I still wanted to say. Mum's last words to me were, "I love you, Susan; go, live your life," with tears streaming down my face and the feel of Mum's bear hug, even with dementia, through the lump in my throat, I said, "Mum, I love you so much," and as the belly sobs were about to burst, Andrew escorted me to the car.

The loss of my mum was quick—too quick. But this loss, along with recovery that I was already implementing because of the Costco incident, caused me to face the grief and years of accumulated loss that I had ignored. Despite the scars I got from her religious expression, I came to realize that for my mum, family was an important core value and she did the best she could with what she knew.

When you do the work, you own the skills. They can't be taken away. They are yours to keep forever.

—Michelle Obama

Normal Self vs. Spiritual Self

If we could travel back in time to ask a much younger version of myself, I would tell you that I thought about becoming a teacher, a psychologist, or a hairstylist. That was on a normal day. Unfortunately for me, as a very young girl, I was also indoctrinated to believe that the world was going to end. And believing that the world was about to end created catastrophic thinking, and it split my worlds in two; this is how I choose to define my past. I had a "normal" life and a "spiritual" life—one life motivated by healthy relationships and another life driven by fear and coercion. If you were to peek into my "normal" life, you would likely come to believe that my life was, for the most part, normal. You might even say my life was even better than normal. I was surrounded by family, siblings, relatives, even grandparents, and our family was well-known and accepted in our community. My "spiritual" life, on the other hand, was a hidden life, a secret life. Being taught that the return of Jesus was imminent—that it could happen any day—along with the fear of the Tribulation to follow enslaved me. It bonded me to fear. Fear literally gripped my soul and short-circuited any belief that I would get to live a full life. I lived most of my childhood and teen years split between these two lives—until my worlds collided and I chose the spiritual self. My life was then driven by fear for decades to come.

It was during this period when I let my spiritual self take over. I attended seminars based on personal development which today can be defined as large-group awareness training sessions (LGATs). Taking part in these seminars culminated in a turning point that changed the trajectory of the next twenty-five years of my life, where I would find myself drawn to prophecy, spiritual warfare, and the supernatural. I believed the Seven Mountain Mandate was Heaven's mandate to bring God's Kingdom to Earth. Today, most of these churches fall under the new banner the New Apostolic Reformation (NAR). I lived it, I breathed it, and I was fully committed to it in spirit, mind, body, and soul.

The process of leaving and disconnecting myself from those bonds was slow for me. I needed to disconnect my attachment hook by hook, bit by bit, piece by piece, and look at what had happened to me so that I could begin to heal and create the future I wanted. I needed to heal the spiritual self that had driven most of my life through fear. Until I did this work, not having the understanding of what all that psychological indoctrination did in me and to me, I would take my "indoctrination template" and lay it over any relationship, group, or workplace that I went into. Taking time away, with support, was where I began to see the power that my past had over me psychologically and physically.

Initially, most of my learning was done through emotional identification by watching, listening, and understanding the stories of other survivors. As I watched documentary after documentary, I identified with those who had either left cults, been victims of LGATs, or self-identified as having experienced religious or spiritual trauma. I could even relate to other woman in narcissistic relationships. I invested time researching religious trauma, cults, undue influence, coercive control, group think, energetics, and attachment styles. I found therapists with whom I could begin to tell my story, outside of any group or religious affiliation.

I didn't know it at the time, but as I took the first step and then another small step, I was beginning to do the work to undo all the years of psychological and social influence that had controlled most of my life. The book *Educated* by Tara Westover was the first book where I could say to myself, *I am not alone! There are others who had been indoctrinated into end-times apocalyptic thinking* (without giving magical answers for how they moved on in life). I could relate to Tara's extremist beliefs, survivalist mentality, and especially her connection to end-times prophecy. Reading Tara's story, I felt like I was being thrown a lifesaver.

Since that time, I've found many other supports: online groups, support groups, educators, coaches, and therapists. Since *Eat, Pray, Love* by Elizabeth Gilbert was released on film, it became a yearly watch. Yes, ask my now-adult children. Since 2020, I've read the book and realized that she too responded to a prophecy (a palm reading) from a toothless man. I could see myself in her journey of spiritual investigation and self-inquiry, as I could relate to her attaching herself to someone—or something—else that seemed to promise what she longed for most.

Fast forward to today, as I continue to heal and demystify my experiences with the supernatural, I have new words—words that give me the language to understand what happened to me and the words I needed to write my story with clarity. These words open doors to a new future. As I share my story, it is my hope that it will help bring understanding to what religious and spiritual traumas can look like when a young child is indoctrinated rather than born into it, and what undue influence can look like and how it impacts a child's sense of self and their hope for the future.

You will read how I began to ask questions unhindered by authoritarian rule and punitive consequences; it was only then that I could begin to test the waters of what I truly believed. Disengaging from all forms of spiritual bypassing, I could see the systems, the people, and the indoctrination for what they were. I processed the good, the bad, and the ugly. You will read about the traumas I experienced, both within and outside of the system. You will also read about how I came to embody the art of falling. In the end, you will see how I learned to accept myself at every stage of my life through a process called integration. Through integration, I've been able to build my coherent narrative, accept both my normal and spiritual self as genuine expressions of my being, and learn to love myself at every stage of my life, even if I wouldn't make those same decisions now.

This Book Is for You

I've written this book for those who want to reclaim their story, their narrative, or their voice, especially when their life has been heavily influenced by another person.

For those who have believed that parts of themselves had to be given away or cut off in order to belong.

For those who have blurred the lines between where they end and someone else begins.

For those who find themselves parroting what they have been told, but inside, they still have questions.

For those who believe that *no* is one of the scariest words to voice.

For those who find themselves scanning their daily prophetic word or horoscope in hopes of getting some clarity about this life.

For those who find themselves attracted to powerful people and powerful groups.

For those who find themselves returning to survival mode again and again.

For those who find themselves sensing the tone of people, rooms, and conversations before they even interact with them.

For those who replay conversations over and over, rewinding, replaying, and rehashing everything long after the event is over.

For anyone still untangling their story and feel stuck in circular thinking—same story, different page.

For those who find themselves questioning their spiritual journey and their relationship with church.

For those who find themselves in an unbalanced power dynamic.

For those who have sensitive, thoughtful, and empathic natures.

I've also written this book as a tool for helping practitioners and professionals who work with individuals who have experienced religious trauma, spiritual abuse, or undue influence. It is my hope that my story will shine a light on the reality that many people experience—the reality of fear, indoctrination, trauma bonding, religious and spiritual trauma, prophecy, and especially end-times prophecy, all of which can massively impact someone's life.

It is my hope that through sharing my story, readers will learn that what is happening in the world today is not a new story, but an old story being presented in new way; that the desire for connection and belonging is a human need; and how that desire can become exploited. And just as a Velcro hook connects to a loop, these types of bonds are not easily pulled apart and require a season of undoing, or deconstructing, in order to be truly free.

How This Book Works

In **part one**, I share my story from the ages of five to twenty-one, where I, as a young girl, was indoctrinated to believe that Jesus was about to return any day, an event called the Rapture, where the true believers would be taken in the blink of an eye, while the "others" would all be left behind. You will read about the event that caused me to step outside of myself, forming a second self, and my trauma bond to prophecy. I share about the points in my life where I experienced bullying, isolation, and risky situations that created vulnerabilities that made me an easy target for power imbalances in relationships and groups, also known as undue influence. You will begin to read about the tug-of-war between my normal self and my spiritual self, which ultimately became a battle, and which side would seemingly win.

In **part two,** I share my story from the ages of twenty-two to forty-four, where I was pulled into the world of personal development in the form of LGATs and my proceeding fallout. You will read about how I reconnected to the church, met my first husband, and found a church that became our home for eight years. In this church, we got connected to the NAR, prophets, *rhema* words, spiritual warfare, prophetic dance, and Kingdom business. We were in it until we weren't.

It's here in part two that I fully give into my spiritual self and allow that fear to drive me to seek patterns and answers in everything but myself; people's opinions, people's thoughts of me, and even signs based on people's clothing choices were all sources of truth that I based every decision off of. My sense of autonomy withered as I attempted to move forward in my life while my childhood trauma remained unrecognized and unprocessed. I remained vulnerable to the effects of struggle, grief, trauma, and accumulated loss, all of which created a vulnerability in my life and left me susceptible to people and groups that promised what I thought I lacked. I was a seeker. I came to believe that I had found answers, meaning, purpose, and that I had finally found my tribe. This seeking was wrapped in promises of lasting transformation as I experienced some of the breakthroughs I sought. It was a cleverly designed and crafted game, but I won't see that yet. I was never the one giving myself an answer.

In **part three**, I share my story from age forty-five to today, where I fully begin the process of detaching and disconnecting myself from all those Velcro hooks. I share about my return to Canada, reconnecting to the workforce, finding non-Christian counselling, and how I began to notice the tug-of-war between my normal self and my spiritual self. You will read about how I met my new husband and what it took for me to use to my natural gifts and talents outside of the church.

I share about what I learned in the holistic realm such as energetics, the nervous system, and how I began to develop a sense of self beyond the confines of the church. This is where I saw and experienced many things I had considered spiritual happening outside the context of the church. Learning new things allowed me to begin to step out of fear and to ask the big spiritual questions. I also share about how integration was my key to healing; integrating memories and connecting true emotions to those events allowed me to make sense of what I had experienced, allowing my brain, body, and emotions to form a new narrative.

Continuing to use the metaphor of threads, I have included **threads I hold** sections. Each of these threads carry a lesson, a voice. While I cannot undo the weaving for someone else, nor live someone else's pattern, I can hold my own threads with care—seeing and appreciating their colour, their texture, and their truth.

These threads I hold sections provide my current perspective on past events and show how I reclaimed my narrative—giving voice to what I wished an adult might have said or done for me. In the earlier chapters, these threads speak to the developing trauma bonds and the guidance I needed at that stage of my life. In the later chapters, the threads offer further context on the fears that were driving me, the ways I was being manipulated, and the pieces I was missing at the time.

I've also included a few of the **prophecies** I've received throughout my life. I have chosen to transcribe the prophecies as they were dictated from the recordings. At times, they may feel disjointed or even chaotic; that is the rhythm of the prophet's voice. I include them not merely as parts of my story but as a window into what has been, what might be, and what continues to unfold today in groups of undue influence—often in the name of God. You will read about the impact prophecy had on my life, my belief system, and the direction I—and by extension, my family—took in ministry, personally and professionally, especially since our business was inextricably linked to the prophetic world.

I've chosen to narrate my story from the stance of a woman reclaiming her power and her voice. My story matters just as your story matters.

My story matters because I matter.
I am absolutely enough.

—Brené Brown

Part One

1

THE BEGINNING OF THE END

I found myself in a familiar environment: a house that was considered a grand home in the 1970s, for it had many rooms with multiple entry points. In some ways, it felt like a giant puzzle that spanned room to room, connected yet divided. Visits with my mum for coffee, a quick stop just to say hello, and moments enjoying ice cream treats while spinning around on the red-covered stools are all memories I have here. In this home, children were given TV time in the library while the adults gathered in the larger living room for spiritual meetings. I knew this home.

I have many memories of going to house meetings, or home church, here as a young child. At these meetings, I was first introduced and then indoctrinated into believing that Jesus would be returning "any day." For me, this "any day" began in the 70s.

In my recollection, I heard the teaching this way. When the Rapture takes place, Jesus would take the born-again believers to Heaven with Him while the rest of the non-believers (which was most of my family) would be left behind to go through the Tribulation period of seven years; then, Jesus would return again, which is known as the Second Coming, and reign for one thousand years. Afterwards, the Last Judgement would take place between those who would be qualified to enter Heaven and those who would be sent to

Hell (where there would be gnashing of teeth for eternity). At the time (and today), there were differing theological viewpoints about the exact order of the events of the Rapture and if it would take place in one or two instances. Regardless of the exact order of events, in my child mind, this belief was the beginning of the end.

This prophecy attached itself to me. I was hooked. It overwhelmed my little brain and body in many ways; as a way to cope, I developed the habit of mouth chewing. I would bite away at the insides of my lips and cheeks, often needing medical attention. Emotions are contagious, and being a sensitive child attuning to the adults around me meant my nervous system was often dysregulated, as messages of impending doom, fear, and terror became deeply rooted within me. I don't believe the adults around me understood that these theological perspectives could plant the seeds of dualistic thinking, disassociation, and for me, fragmentation.

Looking at my life from the outside, one might believe that I was fine; I had connection, understanding, and adult support, and I also had the privilege of being raised in a community surrounded by numerous relatives. My grandfather and grandmother lived only four blocks away from our family home, and as a child, I would spend as much time with them as I could. My grandmother, often with me in tow, would spend afternoons in the small shack in the back of the neighbour's yard creating colorful rugs by weaving strips of recycled fabric. You may have seen similar rugs sold at IKEA. As the other women gathered, I found myself listening to them speak in a language I could not understand (I believe they spoke Slovak). As I heard these unfamiliar words, I felt safe and loved, but I was also curious as to what these women passing shredded fabric back and forth were actually discussing. Did they talk about the latest meal they made? Or was it woman talk about their husbands' latest escapades? I'll never know. I felt a generational bond to these women who worked with their hands and spoke a different tongue, unlike the other type of tongue that I would hear at house meetings, where the words spoken would cause my little body to feel stiff and frozen; here, in this little shack, I felt light and free.

This split in my family deepened the fragmentation within me. It forced me to create and inhabit two worlds. One world was my spiritual world, with my mum and her house meetings, and the second world was my normal world, where I got to enjoy afternoons with my grandma and her group of friends. I had a roof over my head, food on the table, and a warm bed to sleep in. My physical needs were taken care of, but my emotional needs sometimes slipped between the cracks. I was always encouraged to take part in as many outdoor activities and sports as I wanted. By the age of eight, my mum enrolled me in the local swimming club, and by the end of that summer, I won the trophy for most improved. In my normal world, I could play, achieve, and seemingly thrive. One might say that my childhood looked quite normal, except it wasn't. I lived a dualistic life. I had this other world where spiritual mysticism and doomsday prophecy lived and breathed and took up space in my young brain. This space was secret, and it would undermine and dictate my decision making. As I grew older, this secret space would begin to manifest even more and I took on two very different lives.

I learned and adapted to each world by creating a spiritual self and normal self. Each of these selves came with completely different and, most importantly, incompatible belief systems. My spiritual self was completely caught up trying to make sense of the prophecy about the end times and the fate of the world. I began to attach to others in an anxious and disorganized manner. In this world, I lived in quiet despair as my sensitive nature could not withstand the rigid, suppressive, and doomed belief system. My normal self was where my sense of family and community allowed me to gain many life skills that would give me the ability to build resiliency to weather the ups and downs of childhood well into my teen years. When I was my normal self, I seemed to connect with the world around me in a somewhat anxious yet mostly secure way. That is, until an intense experience altered the balance between my two selves—a tipping point.

In a house meeting hosted by one of my mum's close family friends, I would soon discover that I had a date with destiny. This date with destiny wasn't a personal development seminar with Tony Robbins, nor was it a female empowerment prophecy like you'd have with Bishop T.D. Jakes, but it was destined to be a life-altering encounter. This date with destiny wasn't empowering, it was the beginning of my trauma bond to prophecy.

I thought Mum and I were attending just another house meeting, except this would turn out to be *that* meeting where the trajectory of my life would be forever altered—I just didn't know it yet. The house was the same, the people were the same, the red-covered stools were the same, except there was a thick energy in the air and I could feel the hum of anticipation in each room. It felt like there were bubbles all around me and all I had to do was reach out and poke the air to hear one pop. As I turned my head, our eyes met as Simon reached out his hand to greet me. "This is my daughter, Susan," my mum said. I could now clearly see that this man was the source of the buzz throughout the house. "Hi," I replied, refusing to offer him my hand. Simon was a self-taught man of the Word who believed he had been given revelatory insight. I'm not sure if Simon considered himself a prophet, but he believed he knew God's thoughts when it came to me.

As the meeting proceeded, Simon decided that I was ready to accept Jesus as my Lord and Saviour. I had to sit in a chair at the table as Simon attempted to lead me in the Sinner's prayer. This wasn't the game of Simon Says that I knew. As Simon told me to repeat the words, I couldn't do it—the words kept getting stuck in my throat. And when the words didn't come out, it was interpreted as little Susan being disobedient by not complying with what was being asked.

No one asked me what I thought. I had no desire to ask Jesus to take over my life, and I knew I wanted nothing to do with Simon. I can still recall the flood of heat that surged through my body; every nerve ending was on fire, and I felt bewildered and angry at the same time. Conflicting thoughts swirled between wanting to be loved and wanting to run. I wanted to be accepted by God and receive His love, but I was angry that this God was also going to strike the Earth and bring my life to an end before it even had a chance to start. Add in the fear of eternal damnation if I didn't accept Jesus into my heart, all while wanting to be safe. *If I didn't accept Jesus, would I be forever punished? Do I really want to spend eternity in Hell? What would happen to everyone I loved who didn't know Jesus?* It was all too much for little me. I remember the feelings of dread and helplessness filling my body as my mind went blank.

The pressure to conform intensified with threats: "Do you want to be left behind?" "Do you want to be sent to Hell?" "Don't you not want to go to Heaven?" I sat frozen, unable to say anything. The words that Simon wanted me to repeat were now suffocating me as pain, confusion, and anger all expanded deep within me. Simon continued to stand over me as he began to restate the Sinner's prayer, and he asked me, once again, to recite the words to accept Jesus into my heart as my Lord and Saviour. It was all so intense; I couldn't withstand the pressure. I tried as best as I could to repeat the words Simon said and when we finished saying the Sinner's prayer, Simon asked me to raise my hands in the air and give thanks because my life was now "saved." But I couldn't; my body wasn't mine anymore—it was frozen. And when Simon didn't get the response he wanted, he announced to all present that I was being an unthankful child. All eyes were on me, everyone watching, seeing what would happen next. Then, my mum stepped in and—instead of rescuing me from this man, from this situation, from this meeting—she told me in front of everyone that if I could not be grateful, then I could go outside and wait in the car until she was ready to go home.

I remember getting into the back seat of the car and crying for what seemed like hours. Tears of pain and confusion flowed. My cheeks flushed with anger; I felt so mad; it was stuck inside me. Nobody seemed to understand what was happening in my head. It felt like my mum just stepped on my heart, and I couldn't make it go back to how it was. My own mother, embarrassing me in front of everyone—I wanted to disappear. Why didn't she protect me from these people, especially Simon? And I was angry at God. There I said it: "I am angry at you, God." How could this God let me be born only to take away any chance at life? Yet, somehow, I was supposed to receive His free gift of salvation and be grateful at the same time?

As I said those words to myself in the car, I was sure I was doomed to Hell for really saying how I felt out loud. I so wanted to be loved, and yet, I said "God, why do you hate me?" I so wanted to belong and yet I said, "Why was I ever born?" I wanted a future and yet I asked God, "Why did you take away my chance at life?" It was a mixture of pain, rejection, confusion, and torment as I said the words, "God, I hate you," truly believing that God, the creator of the universe, could care less about me and my life. I was put in circumstances where any attempt to have any sense of self, any rights, or any choice was damned.

The psychological stress I experienced that day would form the foundation for each depressive and anxiety episode that would follow for years to come. That day, feeling that I was in a double bind, invited quiet despair to settle into my heart, mind, and body. Hopelessness and helplessness became my unwanted companions. I had just experienced a trauma bond. I became trauma bonded to prophecy, particularly the prophecy of the impending end times. The desires of wanting love, belonging, acceptance, and a future created hooks that inadvertently weaved themselves and attached, through pain, to beliefs that God was angry and judgmental—a God who, for some unknown reason, hated me. This created a conditional sense of being and belonging, which implanted a feeling that there was something intrinsically wrong with me. That day, I cried alone as the feelings of rejection enveloped me and self-hate took root deep in my heart. I felt like my world was just turned upside down by those who should have kept me safe.

As I suffered alone in the car, a family friend, Jenny, came out to see if I was okay. How much time elapsed in the car that day, I'll never truly know, but the scars that were left have lasted a lifetime. Jenny said that she was sure that it would be okay if I went inside now that the meeting was over. I stepped out of my mum's car, and as I did, I believe I left behind any remaining sense of integration I had. That day, my spiritual self took full control; the fear-driven template was laid and it would feed a pattern of abuse where my life, needs, wants, and desires would be minimized as I learned to bypass my nervous system, and in its place, I would give way to the needs, desires, and expectations of those in positions of power over me.

Threads I hold,

Oh, little one. I see how your world is getting turned upside down and whatever secret you think you need to keep from the world is affecting you from the inside out. You don't yet have the words to articulate all the emotions that are going on inside of you. I see you, little one—your pain, your confusion, and your anger that you've turned inward. But, there will be a way to cope better than self-harm. You don't need to punish yourself. You've done nothing wrong. I'm so sorry that the adults around you can't see you or your pain.

Yes, it's true; they only had eyes that focused on themselves and what they wanted. Believe me when I say that I understand how much confusion this causes in your little brain. This trauma reshapes your brain—it changed how you think, how you feel, and begins to turn your world inside out.

Oh dear, little Susan, this has been such a heavy physical and emotional experience for you at such a formative age. I wish I could scoop you up and take you away from there and tell you, "You did nothing wrong." I'd do it in a heartbeat! What has been planted will take root and tether you to this experience and to beliefs that are not true. You do matter, you are worth it, and you will get to live a long life, and you are loved—so loved.

Little Susan, you will have whispers of truth come your way throughout your life, but it will take a little while until the volume is turned down on all the words and emotions that have just consumed you. Eventually, you will hear the whispers, and these whispers will get louder and louder as you give yourself permission to question each situation, each circumstance, especially the event that just took place, and in doing so, you will place responsibility where it is due. Be quick to give yourself permission to question the beliefs that were induced with fear. Trust me when I say that you will learn how to self-adjust, especially when you are given the proper emotional support.

Little one, you will change the narrative of your life; it won't always be this story. I'm here for you. Know that a door will open for you soon, very soon.

The end of the world, the dates, and the prophecies are complete lies—big, huge LIES!

"But it made you stronger."
I was a child—I didn't need to be stronger. I needed
to be safe.

2

DOUBLE DIGITS
AND STILL NO SIGN OF JESUS

As the years progressed, there still was no sign of Jesus's return. However, because of this deeply rooted belief in my spiritual self, I would unconsciously continue to delay the milestones of life just a little bit longer, hoping for more time before the end. On the other hand, my normal self would continue to grow, experience new things, and thrive in the relationships and in the community that I grew up in. My love for sports continued; as I grew, I took advantage of every sport that I was offered: volleyball, basketball, track and field, even badminton was on my list of extracurriculars.

Then, of course, in summer, I focused all my energy and attention on the community pool. In the town of Blairmore, Alberta, our community pool was an outdoor pool along the main road right next to a park and the Kentucky Fried Chicken place. Oh, those Mountain Burgers from KFC! The community pool was also surrounded by magnificent mountains, like Frank Slide, also called Turtle Mountain, the magnificent Crowsnest Mountain, and the Seven Sisters. It truly was picturesque.

Every day, when I wasn't in the water, I was learning and volunteering my time, waiting for the opportunity to become a certified lifeguard. I felt alive when I was in the water—from swimming practice to lessons to volunteering on deck.

As the summer months came to their fullness, so did I; I loved the thrill of accomplishment and seeing the results that came with focus and hard work. When the time arrived that I qualified to take the training to become a certified lifeguard, I did so immediately. No hesitation. I seemed to embody both my choices and my agency; no one would ever know I had another life, another self.

I was doing well in school; learning was high on my priority list. I was voted class president in middle school and was voted team captain for basketball, one of my all-time favourite sports. By age twelve, I would come to win most of the swimming competitions I entered, and I had the trophies and medals to prove it. When I was able to qualify and begin to work as a lifeguard, I knew I wanted more; both small wins and big wins created an appetite for more. By the time I was twenty, I was certified to both teach and examine individuals for their National Lifeguard examination throughout Southern Alberta.

It looked as though that my spiritual self took a back seat to my normal self—life seemed good, I felt good, and one could argue I was brimming with hope.

Our high school started in grade 9 and I embraced this change full on! I had an older brother, Brad, who was also in high school at the same time. Brad was sixteen months older than me, but due to the timing of our birth months, he was two years ahead of me in school. For this girl, that was a plus. With my brother ahead of me, I felt like I had a card in my back pocket that I could pull out and use anytime I needed it. Brad was both smart and athletic. It was exciting to gather for high school sports games and watch Brad front and centre—it made life much more exciting. I was proud to be his little sister and found that it had its benefits; for example, being protected from "others" was a huge bonus.

Since the students from three middle schools came together at one high school, I was able to leave behind outdated friendships and build new ones. My new best friend, Vanessa, was beautiful, smart, funny, and loyal, and we became inseparable. Vanessa and I spent most days together—she was a godsend. My days at Crowsnest High would become filled with sports, academics, and extracurricular activities such as running for school office, and of course, my interest in the opposite sex would begin to take up more and more space as I attempted to navigate the complexities of boy-girl nuances. No one had taught me the delicate dance for when tween boys want to go from friends to boyfriend.

My spiritual self felt like it was becoming a distant memory in high school. I was no longer required to go to house church or prayer meetings, but Jenny continued to be influential in my life, especially since she lived on and off with my family. For the most part, at this stage, I felt that my life was exactly that: my life—my normal self. It was mine to create, and I filled it with sports, friends, school, parties, boys, and in the summer months, lifeguarding and all that came with it. These were good days, and they are positive memories that I hold onto even now.

Threads I hold,
Susan, you are dancing between the normal self and the spiritual self. And as you move, you embody different essences, characteristics, and belief systems. As you continue this back and forth, those who are your relatives will be

conflicted and confused about how you present yourself. Most of them see you as a strong, smart, confident, and outgoing teenager. They didn't see the markings of your spiritual world. Some people would even call you head-strong and that you think you're better than other people. I also believe that some of the girls around you were jealous of you. It will make sense with what is about to come next. When opportunity arises to "put someone in their place," jealousy always tries to point the finger and put you at fault.

Believe you can and your halfway there.

—Theodore Roosevelt

3

THEN, LIFE CHANGED—AGAIN

During the summer of grade 11, life as I knew it would change again, taking a dramatic turn and leaving me feeling as though the rug had been pulled out from underneath me. It was a summer of firsts. My brother graduated the previous year, and I would be entering the school year, for the first time, alone. I had my first serious boyfriend, Dillon, except that didn't go so well—it always goes back to those boy-girl nuances I wasn't taught, especially the ones that teach a girl how to end a relationship well. I was left to navigate feelings of likes, dislikes, what feels right, and what doesn't, all while trying to end my relationship. Dillon, however, was tall, dark, and handsome, and that kept me locked in, especially because he was also athletic and popular among the girls. Yet, on the relationship level, the only thing Dillon and I had in common were power plays, that push-pull relationship dynamic: who's in charge, who's breaking up with who, I want you, I don't want you. It was so confusing, but I was hooked. Back then, I accessed my power by making choices; when I made the decision that something was over, it was over, except it wasn't over. I didn't know how to end things well.

By the time I returned to school that fall, a group of girls had my name on their hit list, and to make matters worse, I had a returning friend from my childhood who quickly became popular at our school, and they hated that I was associated with him. I had no idea how to navigate these dynamics, e.g., what to do when a friend becomes interested in being more than friends, how to read flirting queues, what to do with those queues. The climax of this mixture erupted at a house party. Two boys were physically fighting; it started with one guy jumping another, slamming his fist into his face, and I was the apparent reason for it. I was later told that my childhood friend was about to ask me to go out with him, except I had my sights on another boy. The fight started, but I was completely unaware as to why it started. Next thing I knew, another girl is yelling at me, "You bitch! You wanted this to happen!" *What? How could things get so turned upside down in an instant, at one party?* I remember getting into my car after the fight and the girl who was hosting the party came to my window and said, "Susan, this wasn't your fault. You didn't do this—they did." Tears were already stinging my eyes as I said, "Ya, I know," but inside, it felt like I had gotten into the fist fight myself.

This event triggered something in me, something much deeper than the boy-girl thing; this event retriggered the con-fusion, punishment, and ostracization that I experienced in my spiritual self, which always started when I didn't see the queues or meet the expectations of those around me. Once again alone, I had no words to describe what just happened to me, nor did I have the support I needed to help me pro-cess these climactic events. So, this trauma took root, and this would become another year of firsts.

That year, I went into my first deep depression and I gained forty pounds before Christmas. It was the first year I would win and then withdraw from school counsel. It was the first year that my best friend Vanessa and I would spend less time together, as her life was taking her away from school. It was the first year I began to miss class, let my grades decline, and allow myself to quit trying. I would go home, go to my room, and crawl into bed before the sun would set. It was the first year I began to spend extended periods of time in my mind, creating, on purpose, an imagined fantasy world where I could escape my pain.

Today, this coping style can be identified as a type of maladaptive daydreaming; it's a disassociate state that people who experience trauma can create in their minds to help them survive. Surviving this experience took the bulk of my focus, time, and energy. But what I was waiting for, what I was hoping for, were three things. First, for someone, anyone, to really see me. Second, that this someone would ask me to share what I was feeling, asking me questions to find out what was happening to me. Thirdly, that this someone would take notice of what was going on around me and mirror back to me the social assault I just experienced. But no one did. And once again, the universe seemed to tell me that my needs, my feelings, and my life didn't matter, and I was left to wonder if God was punishing me.

Threads I hold,

It wasn't your fault! You are not at fault! I wish you could have let the words that young girl said to you that night sink in. Yes, life lessons can be knee scraping at times, but this is ridiculous. This isn't a lesson that life is trying to teach you; girls can be mean, boys can be mean, put that together and it's a big bully that needs to be addressed! The fact that no adult around you stepped in or stepped up—so wrong! The fact that you disappeared and no one noticed you were missing—again, wrong! Yes, it was the early 80s, and life for most is hopefully different now, but I'm looking at you and what you lived through.

You, Susan, had the ability to survive even this. You used creativity, you used maladaptive daydreaming, and your fantasy world allowed you to survive that season. You made it through; yes, weathered, beaten, and a lot less self-confident, but you made it through. In your future, you will learn the power of remembering positive life experiences, that through the act of remembering and recalling positive experiences, you can give yourself both the strength and the empowerment to move forward.

Remember your successes, your small wins, and your big wins. Understand that as you do, you are helping your body remember that you can, that you are able, and that you will overcome. No young girl should have to go through this experience alone. My heart breaks for you and yet there is a glimmer of hope I feel for you because I know you make it through, and I am here on this side cheering for you. Next time—boxing gloves!

"Whatever doesn't kill you makes you stronger"—bullshit.

—Susan Stirling

4

TWO WRONGS DON'T MAKE A RIGHT

It would be in my final year of high school that I would see my two worlds collide. I no longer had the energy, nor could I muster up the courage, to try out for any school sports teams. I withdrew from any classes that were not necessary to obtain my diploma, and I enrolled in correspondence courses, avoiding anything and anyone associated with the event of the previous fall.

This was also the year when I welcomed my spiritual self back into my life with open arms. Jenny, our long-time family friend and the young woman who came out to the car to see if I was okay after the Simon incident, was about to become my new safe person. I felt safe when I was with Jenny—I could ask her any questions about life or God. At this time, Jenny was living in another city, and I had the opportunity to visit her since my brother and his friend were going to a music concert there. As was customary, Jenny was actively involved in her church community, and when I arrived after greeting me with a warm hug, Jenny invited me to the church meeting that evening. "This is a meeting where there will be young people," she said. And having endured one of the most difficult years of my life, I accepted: "Yes, that would be nice," I responded. And with those words, off to church we went.

The meeting took place in the church basement, and like most church meetings, we began with worship. As the guitarist began to sing, he invited us to close our eyes. As I followed his lead, closing my eyes, I could feel something stirring within. Here I was, in a spiritual environment again, but this time, it felt different. The atmosphere was touching the deepest part of me, opening something I had buried. Everything I was feeling began to spill out. Before I knew it, I was belly sobbing—the kind of sobbing that happens uncontrollably when unprocessed experiences that were being held down build up enough energy to erupt. I found myself being escorted to a side room with the pastor's wife, Jenny, and another young girl and they helped me find a seat.

For the next few hours, I opened the doors of my heart and allowed my grief to be seen and felt. I let go. I let out the secrets I kept inside, I uncovered what I kept hidden, and as the words came up, I gave voice to what had happened to me. These women gave me the space, time, comfort, and support I needed. Finally, adults and my peers began to mirror back the compassion and empathy I so desperately needed, as if to say, "I see you, I hear you." Tissue after tissue, I shared everything about the previous year—the good, the bad, and my truth in it all. This act of kindness, that someone noticed my pain and responded with concern, was the kind of support that I needed but never received from anyone around me. It was only after I had no more tears left that I was offered their perspective about relationships, boy-girl dynamics, and mean girls. Perspectives that stated, "Yes, you might have done that, but it wasn't all your fault," "You didn't deserve that," "Girls can be so mean," and "God is still here for you, let Him comfort you now." As they spoke these words to me, I could feel the weight of false guilt and false responsibility being lifted off my chest and for the first time in a long time, my breath found my belly.

That night, in that place, for the first time since the previous summer, I felt a glimmer of hope, and the grief that I had been carrying was replaced with a kind of joy that makes you believe in new beginnings. I wondered if I had just encountered the grace that they sang about in worship, God's grace, and I wondered, even if it would take a miracle, if maybe this light would chase away the darkness within me. Maybe, just maybe, God didn't hate me after all. Maybe I did matter. And this thinking changed everything for my spiritual self. A small spark of hope flickered in me—maybe God did love me after all. And if He truly loved me, maybe He wanted good things for me, even if I didn't know how much time was left.

Threads I hold,
Susan, if I could give you the knowledge we have now, you would know that trauma happens when there is an overwhelming sense of danger, powerlessness, or fear. And that healing happens when a safe space is made where the pain can be brought up and grief can be shared, as a voice is given to what one experienced. This space is where support and safety are sacred and honoured without judgement, and these moments become turning points. This isn't a kind of divine intervention, but the act of being seen, heard, and accepted by other humans. Through healing, people obtain emotional clarity, and that enables self-discovery. When pain and grief are able to be digested in a way that leads to a renewed sense of hope, possibilities emerge. You've confused human kindness for God's grace. Healing is a right, not a gift. Watch and see what happens next.

Trauma is a result of an overwhelming sense of danger, powerlessness, and fear. Healing is a result of feeling safe, empowered, and supported.

5

LET THE LIGHT SHINE—ONCE AGAIN

After that evening at church with Jenny and the pastor's wife, I felt as though I had opened the window to let in the fresh spring air after a long winter—the kind of air that made me want to focus outward rather than inward. My heart felt light again, just like I felt with my grandmother and her friends in the shack in the neighbour's backyard, and the air carried a hint of new beginnings.

The summer of 1984 arrived at my doorstep with an invitation to begin again. My body knew summer, I knew summer, and in the sunlight, I remembered I could thrive.

What I didn't realize was that I still wasn't making long-term plans; I was just existing, month by month, year by year. I could only see the short term; I couldn't envision what my life might be like five, ten, or twenty years down the road. When my peers talked about post-secondary school or what they wanted for their career paths, I found myself with blinders on. It didn't occur to me in the least that my childhood trauma, a.k.a. my spiritual self, was impacting my ability to see. I only felt knots in my stomach when it came to thinking about what might come next. There was a mounting anger growing inside me, feeling as though I'd been lied to, duped as they say, because I was in my late teens and if I heard "Jesus is returning" out of my mum's mouth again, I swear I was going to break something. In my high school yearbook,

I wrote that I wanted to be a human resources manager since my cousin was the vice president of human resources at a major company at that time. That is how I thought of the future: I mirrored those I admired.

It's important to remember that my two selves didn't talk. They didn't help each other. My normal self was confounded as to why I couldn't decide on a vocation and then act on it. *I had accomplished so much as a lifeguard, so why couldn't I figure this out?* I didn't make the distinction that my spiritual self was putting the mental breaks on. The belief that I was still looking for the end was still mostly unconscious. My thoughts around Jesus's return would only be activated in certain environments and under certain conditions. Yet, deep inside, when I had moments of hopeful possibility, when I gave myself to the curiosity I was feeling, I would find myself thinking about becoming a psychologist, a teacher, or a hairstylist. When I asked my parents, my father told me I should become a secretary, and my mum hoped I'd become a nurse since she would have done that if she had had the chance.

By the end of that summer, I had made my choice: I followed my boyfriend at the time, Greg, who I had met at a beach party. Greg was attending college in Lethbridge and so I decided to join him. I spent the next year in college doing an administration certification. Other than learning how to do a few things that assists a person in business, what I was learning was completely different from following my curiosity. It was that year that I decided that maybe I could get married before Jesus returned.

As the academic year came to an end, summer plans could once again begin, and I wanted nothing more than to be home and spend the summer lifeguarding. As I returned home, it was as though muscle memory took over and my self-confidence quickly regained strength. I decided to make some changes to take back my life. I ended my relationship with Greg, and once again, the relationship didn't end well, but I focused my energies on allowing myself the freedom of a fresh start.

By the end of the summer of 1985, I was nineteen years old, and even though my personality leans towards stability sprinkled with adventure, I felt the desire to give city life a try. And as I started city life, I did it with some support. I spent my first few months in Calgary living with an aunt who I had always been fond of. Aunt Melinda was a kind, caring, and thoughtful woman who always welcomed me with open arms. Once I found full-time employment as the receptionist at the Calgary Philharmonic Orchestra, I was encouraged to move out on my own. I found a suite in a home not far from my aunt's that allowed me to keep some familiarity in my life. That year working as the receptionist at the philharmonic was a year of discovery. My normal self had once again emerged and I gladly gave myself over to it. I was fully engaged in my life and completely enjoying this new opportunity.

At the philharmonic, I would meet new people and become friends with Juliana, who would become a long-time friend. The skills that I learned and applied as a lifeguard gave me a skillset that opened doors for me. My sense of self was growing again, and my self-confidence came back stronger than ever. I was fully in my normal self. The year went so well that Juliana and I made the decision to spend the next year on an adventure together. Australia was calling and we wanted to answer that call! Caught in the momentum of the situation, I made the easy decision to move back home to work as a lifeguard and save the money I needed for our big adventure. Life seemed full of possibilities and any thought of Jesus, or His return, seemed but a distant echo.

Threads I hold,
There are still days when I wonder what life would have been like if my normal self had full reins throughout my whole life. What would I have done? Who would I have become? What career path would I have chosen? Mirroring life choices are much different than being able to follow one's curiosity on the pathway to finding purpose. What would life have felt like living fully without the dread of impending doom and the weight of judgement over my head?

Moments of reflection and grief can still creep up in the most unexpected places. Zoom calls with others my age, hearing how they carved out their careers, or listening to retirees talk about their retirement when I am finding my stride in the second half in life opens the door to questions, to wonder where life would have taken my normal self. And then I stop. I reground myself. I breathe in deeply and exhale slowly, and as I do, I choose to believe that life is as life is. I cannot change my past, but I can, as much as life allows, author my story from here. To my normal self, I want you to know that you have given me much resilience, much tenacity, even grit, and the courage I needed to take back the narration of my story. Thank you for having the courage to keep stepping out.

I heal out loud so others don't have
to suffer in silence.

—Natalia Rachel

6

THE TIPPING POINT

Our Australia trip didn't go according to plan. We booked our tickets to leave on October 13, 1986: We were to board a flight from Calgary to Vancouver where we would catch a CP Air flight to Australia. However, before our departure, Juliana contracted a medical condition that would keep her from traveling. Nothing felt right about travelling on my own, and as the date approached, I began to feel the fear rising every time I thought about it. The call of adventure was being drowned out by my mounting anxiety. With a few days remaining, I found myself begging to remain in Canada and not have to face travelling on my own. By the time I was at the airport with my mum, sister, and young niece, I couldn't stop the tears from coming as I pleaded to not have to travel on my own. They tried to assure me that my tears were just travel jitters and that I would be fine. "It's nerves, that's all—you'll be fine," Mum said. "You have the names and numbers of the people in Sydney, make sure you contact them." But her words didn't bring the answer I was hoping for. All I could think was that maybe from the outside they thought I looked fine, but I knew I was not okay.

Looking back at this experience, I'm sure that my family had seen my self-confidence blossom over the last year and believed that I could handle anything that came my way, but what they didn't know was that travelling on my own—

navigating airports, travel routes, and youth hostels—outweighed my confidence and my skillset. I still had a lot of skepticism believing that I could carry out this adventure on my own. Making my way to college was one thing, navigating Calgary was another, but guiding myself through another continent seemed impossible. I hadn't developed enough skills to be travelling solo. But go, I did. The knot in the pit of my stomach would remain there until I returned to Canada.

I would come to learn that the defining feature of my trip to Australia would be the sheer amount of yellow and red flags that I was completely ignorant of. I hadn't any idea of what to do once I got to Australia; I hadn't booked a hostel, I hadn't made any phone calls, no ideas, no plans—only red flags.

I arrived in Australia exhausted. I recall walking out of the airport with my travel backpack and seeing a taxi, and as I got into the taxi, the driver asked me where I wanted to go. I had no destination to give him. I said I needed to find a youth hostel and asked if he knew where one would be. I'm so grateful that that taxi driver was a kind-hearted man—my life was in his taxi, literally.

Once we got to the hostel, the taxi driver went to the front desk on my behalf. "Hiya mate, is there a room for this young lady?" the taxi driver asked. "No, sorry mate, we're chock full," the front desk person responded. Then, he turned to me and asked, "If you want to take a shower, you can." *Oh God, I must stink. I hadn't thought of the flight, the stress, and the smell.* "No, thank you," I said. There was no way in hell I was about to take off any piece of clothing until I got where I needed to be, stench or no stench. The hostel worker and the taxi driver talked; phone calls were made on my behalf.

Next thing I knew, they had found me a bunk in another hostel. The kind-hearted taxi driver and I got back into his taxi and off we went. This time, when we arrived at the next hostel, I went in alone. And no, I still didn't shower. It would be a few days before I called the family from Sydney that my mum had given me the name and number for. Don and his family welcomed me warmly, but I still couldn't control my nerves about the whole situation.

I had dreamed of going to Australia for over a year, but now that I had arrived, I felt at risk. My at-risk feelings became loud and clear when I answered an ad to work at a horse ranch a few hours outside of Sydney. After a short phone interview, I was given the opportunity to come and see the ranch and I was even offered the position over the phone if I wanted it. *That was easy!* I still didn't recognize red flags. My stay with the family who had ties to Canada was about to come to an end, and so Don drove me to meet the man I just had spoken with over the phone. I can recall being greeted at the front door by the man who I spoke with, and as I entered the house, the first bedroom door was open and I quickly scanned the room to find two people laying in bed watching TV. Luckily, Don agreed to wait in his car until I gave him the signal that all was well. I was offered a seat at the kitchen table and as I took a seat, I noticed how uncomfortable I felt. Everything in me was signaling me to run, but I didn't; I sat there as if I was glued to the chair. Thankfully, Don came to the front door and when I heard his voice, I stood up and asked if we could speak privately. We went back into his car, and I told him I didn't want to stay. Don assured me everything was going to be okay; "Just give it a go," he said. The next thing Don did was open the glovebox where he kept a "tool" and said, "If you want, you can take this with you, you know, to help you feel safe." I remember thinking that if I took that tool, it might be used against me!

And with those words, I watched as Don drove away and I could feel with every ounce of my being that something terrible was just set in motion. It would be the last time that I saw Don or his family. I was now faced with survival. *How could I have said yes to this? How could Don just leave me here?* I needed to find a way to get myself out of this mess. My brain and body were on fire; it was as if every nerve ending was ignited, burning with panic and confusion, except I wasn't listening. Just like when Simon asked me to sit down in that kitchen chair to "get saved," every nerve ending was on fire. All I could do was think about how I would survive this. How could someone leave me here like this—again?

My new employer, Ray, spent the next few hours trying to convince me that I was safe and that this would work out if I gave it a try. I sat at the kitchen table for what seemed like hours as Ray offered me tea to try to ease my discomfort. Finally, Ray was able to coax me to the living room where he began to relax and as he did, he began to share a sad story about his wife passing and how he had let things go since. Then, he began to share how his previous worker, who was also a Canadian, ended up getting romantically involved with him. Red Flag! Hell! Red Light!

It was all too much. Hearing these words scared me and I began to cry that same kind of belly cry that I did in the church meeting in my late teens. My distress was obvious. Nothing would settle me, and my distress continued. Ray offered, "Okay, let me take you to the motel in the next town, think on it, and I'll give you a call in the morning. If you still want the job, it's yours." Looking back, I'm grateful that in all the scenarios of what could have happened that day, Ray chose to offer me kindness and a ride. When we arrived in the small town nearby, the motel we found had rooms available. "Room for one," I said. Once I got the key to the room, Ray said, "Remember, I'll be giving you a call in the morning." And with that, we parted. I thought I had gotten myself to safety, but it was about to be a long night.

I wouldn't have left that room if I didn't need food. The motel room felt safe, even just for one night, but I was starving. I gathered my backpack and set off to the food store a few blocks away. Upon returning to the motel, I was walking along the veranda and the room beside me had the door open. One of the people inside that motel room made a comment about the Canadian flag I had sewn on my backpack. From his accent, I could tell he was Australian, but I pretended I didn't hear him and quickly got to my room and closed the door.

Processed food never tasted so good. I was famished. I ate everything I bought and tried to watch some TV, but my mind was focused on how I could get myself back to Sydney. I wrapped myself in the bedspread fully dressed waiting for the room next door to quiet down, but it never did. Now the noise moved onto the balcony outside my window. *What were they saying? Talking to a who? A father?* I tiptoed over to the curtain and with the lights out, I slowly pulled back the curtain just enough to peek out and see if I what I was hearing was actually true. To my shock, I saw one of the men talking to an older man dressed in what looked like a priest's robe, and as I did, I could hear the man say, "It's okay, Father, come in—she'll take care of you." Suddenly, one of the Australians turned towards my window and I jumped back. I wasn't sure if he saw me or not, but the pounding on my door was a dead giveaway. "Come on, Canadian! Open the door, I need a light. Come on, I saw you!" My heart pounded in my throat, and I panicked. I grabbed my things and looked for a way to escape, but there wasn't one; the front door was the only way in and out. I tried to lift the phone to get to the front desk, but no one was answering. I was sure I was going to die. I got on my knees facing the front door, shaking from head to toe, tears streaming down my face. Then, I began to bargain, it was more than a sales pitch—it was a survival tactic. I bargained with God saying, "If you get me out of this, then I will do whatever you want me to," feeling as though life itself was on the line. I would do whatever it was God wanted me to do. "Just please, get me out of this!" I said out loud. I was stuck, literally glued to that motel floor.

Then, as suddenly as it started—it ended. Through the noise, the pounding on the door, and the pounding of my heart, I heard another man's voice, "Come on, man, leave her alone." And as he walked away, he tapped on my window, "Goodbye, Canadian, you could have had some fun." I was outside myself, watching this take place. It felt as though I was watching a scene from a movie, except it was my life. When I came back to myself, the room was silent, except my entire being was electrified.

The rest of the night, once I was able to move, I swaddled myself in the bedspread and prayed that morning would come. Morning couldn't come soon enough, but it came. It was only in the morning that someone answered at the front desk. Then, my motel phone rang. It was Ray. After telling Ray that I was not going to work for him, I told him that I was going to take a bus back to Sydney and go back to the hostel I was staying at before. He told me that buses don't run on Sundays from this town and that he happened to be going back to Sydney himself. I wanted out. I needed to get away. I took Ray up on the offer for a ride into Sydney. I hadn't thought of checking on the bus, probably from the shock I must have been in. Such a red flag. Ray arrived to pick me up and as I walked by the next room, the door was wide open. As I passed the doorway, I heard their smug laughter. *I hate this place, I hate these people, and I desperately want to go home.*

As soon as Ray's vehicle arrived at the hostel, I didn't hesitate; I opened the door to his vehicle as fast as I could and ran from the car and never looked back. Once inside the safety of the hostel, the next thing I did was place a call to Canada. I wanted to go home with my entire being, but for some reason, I felt as though I needed to ask permission. Using the hostel pay phone, I placed a call, and my father answered, "Hello?" "This is a collect call, would you accept the charges?" "Yes," I could hear my father say. And before he could say anything, I took the lead, "Hi Dad, it's Susan," I said through a teary voice. My voice quivered as I began to cry harder, "Dad, something's happened and I want to ask if I can come home. I know I haven't been here for the full year, but I can't do this anymore. Can I come home?" I heard concern in my dad's tone as he said, "Of course you can," and with those words, a glimmer of hope began to rise within me. But beneath that glimmer of hope, there was a certainty that I felt: I hated this place. I had already written and sealed the Christmas cards I was going to send back home and taking a pen on the back flap of every envelope, I wrote, "Looks like I'll be home for New Years!"

I spent the next few weeks in Coffs Harbour where I would meet up and spend Christmas with Danielle. I had met Danielle at the youth hostel in Sydney when I first arrived and we became travel buddies. Once I escaped the horse ranch, Danielle and I spent every day together until I travelled home, and she even came to Sydney to see me off at the airport. Danielle was a gift from Heaven, a godsend, my little English angel, and yet, when I could prepare to board my plane, I couldn't say goodbye fast enough.

Threads I hold,

Wow, Susan! Here you are in your twenties, but why in the world doesn't anyone around you recognize the yellow flags, the red flags, or hear the warning bells when it comes to you? This part of your story is bizarre, unnatural, and completely surreal, but it was your reality. By the time you returned home, you would lose over thirty pounds and stopped menstruating the whole time you were gone; these were some of your body's red flags. Holy f@ck, Susan. It makes complete sense why you did not travel alone for the next twenty years. It makes complete sense why you keep the lights on and put a chair at the door when you're alone. These events impacted your life profoundly. Your inability to see red flags will keep you attaching to relationships, groups, and systems in an unhealthy way and it will keep you in a constant search for approval from outside sources.

It's as though you only wanted to look through rose-coloured lenses that highlighted the positive, as if you were trying to use an eraser to eliminate anything negative. You may have felt short-term emotional relief, but doing that keeps you hooked; you'll need to numb one way or another. Your sense of joy in life gets muted when you don't give voice to the pain. It doesn't create health. You will learn that honouring your story in a safe space, with a safe person, can be a powerful healing tool. It's part of building a coherent narrative from a narrative that is currently only fragments.

Writing out your story will bring much clarity to your experiences and the resulting patterns in your life. Writing your story will also help you create a new narrative that moves your life forward, but for now, know that I know just how much Australia was a tipping point in your life.

You are a survivor, Susan. There has been something inside you that kept you searching. You never give up. I know that you feel like your normal self is now beginning to feel like your spiritual self—it's getting difficult to see the separation inside of you. When you arrive back home, you will be met with silence as you try to share what just happened to you. You will be told, "That was then, this is now; you're safe." No one will make space for your struggle or your grief. This experience will be minimized. Yes, you were home, yes, you were safe. People around you will notice your tan, your weight loss, but they won't notice the change inside of you. But I do, I did.

In the coming season of your life, I wish I could tell you that this trauma, having gone unprocessed, will start short-circuiting your life. You will have great starts, but erratic and dramatic endings that don't go the way you'd hope they would. This is a symptom of your trauma; feelings that are buried alive never die. You have great opportunities, new jobs, new relationships, new friendships, but then something inevitably happens, and all your effort goes to waste.

… it dictated a certain direction my life took.
That I just felt that it was this huge error in
judgement that sort of marked me, and all my
decisions. And I felt such shame that I let him do that.
It was like he took my voice that day.
Just when I was about to start finding it.

—Laura Madden, *She Said* (in reference to abuse
from Harvey Weinstein)

Part Two

$$\overline{7}$$

BREAKTHROUGH

After my return from Australia, I once again found myself living in Calgary, but this time, I was in search of something—more of a feeling than a new understanding. I desperately wanted to have that feeling of being alive again. That feeling that some people call thriving. I felt as though a cloud followed me wherever I went. A bit like the children's book character Winnie the Pooh; on the cloudy days, when the sun forgot to shine and the sky forgot how to be blue, where he didn't feel like humming, he didn't feel like honey, he didn't feel much like anything at all.

As my eyes opened to greet the day, I felt as though a blanket of grey had settled in and was here to stay. Quiet despair filled my thoughts and my lungs. My breath kept getting caught somewhere halfway between dread and numbness. I was in a continuous state of transition, where instability and change were my only companions. Yet, my insides craved some kind of stability. It was during this period of searching and transition that I would be introduced to a course by our close family friend, Iris, who happened to serendipitously come into my life again.

Iris would share stories about a personal development course she just took that completely changed her life. This course gave her the answers that she was searching for and now she herself would say her life was completely transformed.

Actually, Iris looked transformed! It wasn't just lipstick and rouge; this newness seemed tangible. There was a light in her eyes and a confidence she wore—all the things that I felt I was missing, and I desperately wanted what she had.

"It's an experiential course, so I can't share too much, but believe me when I say it's something that once you experience it, you'll never be the same. It will change your life. As you can see, it's changed mine for the better." I trusted Iris and I trusted that she wanted the best for me; it was as though an invisible thread pulled me to her.

Iris met me at the door as I walked into my first introductory session. As I stepped across the threshold and entered the room, everything seemed to have its place. We took our seats and a short middle-aged man took the small stage; I have to admit, he reminded me of a car salesman. As the presentation began, rather than keeping my eyes front and centre, I found myself people watching. I noticed the nodding of heads that seemed to allude to the fact that maybe they knew something I didn't? Maybe they had some inside information I didn't yet have. My brain kept getting scattered, like it was trying to take everything in all at once. I told myself to focus, and as I did, I heard the words, "Guilt is simply action and belief out of alignment; you either change the action or change the belief. It's that simple."

What? Huh? Can you repeat that? My mind took off running again; I just couldn't seem to wrap my mind around what he just said. *Hmm, they must know something I don't*, a voice inside me said. And as I looked around the room seeing all the heads bobbing in agreement, I said to myself, *They must.*

Not fully recognizing yet what a red flag was, I leaned into trust and embraced the unknown. I trusted Iris and I wanted what she had. Next thing I knew, I was signing up for the five-day course, starting with Level One. *I can do this. Levels, I can do levels.* I had that familiar feeling again, it was subtle, yet purposeful, as I imagined my normal self when I said yes to lifeguard training. This could be like that except version 2.0, and as I pictured my "next level," something inside me began to rise.

I have always considered myself a lifelong learner. I love that about myself. I have an appetite to learn about topics that I find intriguing: people stuff, relational dynamics, and finding answers to the whys like why humans do what they do. Like with exquisite chocolate, I'm always on the hunt for more.

The day I walked into my first session, I was *all in.* I was introduced to a group of people that were about to become my community. Middle-aged women who were not satisfied with the status quo, seekers, career people, salespeople, realtors, office workers, even business owners formed this group, and two of us twentysomethings. We were a mix, but that would become part of the magic; we were seeking breakthroughs and transformation, and it began right there in Level One.

The exercises that we weren't supposed to talk about— the visualizations, guided meditations, stretches, and personal challenges—were all designed to help us breakthrough, which means "get to the next level" or "create lasting change" by creating a shift in perception. Breakthrough is about a sudden or profound change in how someone views themselves, their life, or their patterns. We could breakthrough if we chose to let it happen. It's a transformative moment where something internal that was previously stuck, hidden, or blocked becomes visible, understood, and often released.

As I experienced these transformational events, it wasn't what happened in each seminar that stuck out; it was the emotions they caused to erupt within me. The lifeboat exercise evoked feelings of vulnerability, anxiety, and an overwhelming sense of responsibility, as though someone's future depended on my answer. Being told to stand in front of each person, to pause, reflect, and then tell them my final answer—my decision as to whether they got my vote to live or not—was too much. In this exercise, twentysomething Susan was one of the lucky ones. People voted for me to live, and that meant I got a seat on "the lifeboat."

This was my first experience outside of a religious group where I felt such a strong sense of belonging. I felt a sense of family even though I was only in my early twenties. Being connected to a group that was built on transformation, who sought to support me to become the best possible version of myself, was outside of any type of relationship dynamic I had experienced before. I don't know if I was being driven by my normal self or my spiritual self. I didn't quite know what to think or believe for years to come. This was a whole new concept for me: connection, personal development, and spirituality—a powerful threefold cord. My spiritual self was drawn to breakthrough and creating meaning, not just on a emotional level, but almost as if was a spiritual awakening. When I thought of connection, it was as though these people really saw me, understood me, and had my back. And with levels to attain, my goal-oriented normal self was focused on the prize. It was an intoxicating mix.

I would spend the next three years working my way through the levels, finally securing a spot to become a facilitator in the program. This showed me that my desire for goal attainment had been a strength, but it could also become a vulnerability, a hooking point. Once I'd set my sights on a goal, it was hard to get my focus off it, and in doing so, I missed or ignored a lot of red flags. I may not have fully understood red flags conceptually, but after my experience in Australia, I had begun to learn to trust my internal warning bells. However, I was still bypassing my intuition.

By the end of those three years, I was caught in an emotional and physical relationship with the presenter from the first night when Iris invited me. The same man who was not only giving me the vibes of a car salesmen, but he was twenty-five years my senior. Did he feel guilty having a relationship with someone who could be his daughter, you might be asking? Back then, I would ask you the following question in response, "What is guilt?" According to the definition I had been taught and internalized, the likely answer would be "just change the belief."

No matter how hard I tried to change my belief system, to think differently, I couldn't seem to get myself to cross the finish line, and by not crossing the line, I felt like the biggest failure of all time. In my thinking, I only had myself to blame. Rather than seeing all the cognitive dissonance that I was experiencing for what it was, I put more pressure on myself and finally psychologically broke. By handing over any sense of self in the name of self-exploration, by suspending my personal values in the name of new thought, and by redefining my personal boundaries around this new perspective in which "I created everything that happened to me," I snapped. *Was this my transformation, my breakthrough moment? Was I responsible for everything that happened to me? Did I create my experience regarding the end-of-the-world prophecy?*

I had switched one form of indoctrination for another. Except this time, instead of believing that God was creating my world, I was responsible for everything in my life. *Was my outer world a reflection of my internal world?* My mind could not contain so many contradictory thoughts. I didn't know what cognitive dissonance was, but I had been immersed in an environment that had me stuck between my old beliefs and the new beliefs they were presenting. The psychological stress felt like my beliefs were wrestling with reality, my thoughts were tripping over each other, my emotions froze mid step, and then came the *wait, what?*

Over the three years, my brain had had enough of the up-down, push-pull, back-and-forth teeter-tottering that my mind created an emotional overload and my brain felt like it was about to break. Instead, it went numb. Numbness didn't know what to do next, but the easiest choice was to return to where I found the most support; I went back to my spiritual self. My life was about to shift again—if I was choosing my spiritual self, choosing to return to God, then I would also need to return home. Those conclusions seemed to go hand in hand.

It felt as though I was walking through fog: All sounds were muted and edges became blurred and distant. I'd felt this feeling before; life was beginning to dull again. I began to place one foot in front of the other, but I couldn't see how this was going to end well. First step, I would leave the three-year relationship with the man twenty-five years my senior. Second step, I walked away from my felt sense of support I had built in this community. Third step, I functioned like a robot. Except, instead of trying to disconnect my mind and body by creating a void between my head and my heart, I created a vacuum of all feelings, thoughts, and emotions, which was quickly filled with unprocessed trauma: It was like accumulated loss, repressed grief, and psychological stress on steroids.

Threads I hold,

Susan, you don't know this yet, but you've just experienced something that will later be recognized as mind dynamics, which is defined as "inducing states that create imbalances within the brain and can manifest as mania." Dr. John Hunter's hypothesis is eye-opening and his book Manufacturing Mania is a must-read. You will also come to meet and read Anne L. Peterson's book Is This a Cult about her time working for Werner Erhard and her twenty plus years inside a popular self-help organization. You will come to have many of the answers to the questions you have been pondering.

For these past few years, your feelings, your beliefs, and your actions have been incongruent and that has created accumulated stress not only in your life but in your brain. The combination of past traumatic experiences that were swept under the rug and the psychological stress that you are now experiencing is going to put you off balance in a way that will cause your brain to snap. Thankfully, support will come quickly, medical help and qualified help that will assist you. By starting to get the help you need, along with proper medication, counselling, and support, you will get back on your feet quickly, almost too quickly. You'll be hooked again by human kindness before you have a chance to see it. I want you to know, Susan, that you have the skills—they are still in you. Your ability to persevere, to learn, to find answers and solutions—next time, with checks and balances—are going to help you create health, peace, and stability in your life. You will begin to resource yourself from the inside out rather than continually looking for reassurance from others. But buckle up; it's going to be a bit of a rocky ride until then.

In the future, you will learn from people like Steven Hassan, Rachel Bernstein, Janja Lalich, and many others. You will learn about undue influence, authoritarian groups, and new age concepts. Educating yourself on this, with support, therapy, and coaching, will help you sort out what you believe and, most importantly, you will have the courage and the tools to take back your narrative and your life. Before I go today, let me mirror back this truth to you: You are right; what you have experienced is a mindf@ck.

Half a truth is often a great lie.

—Benjamin Franklin

8

HOME

Returning home wasn't my first choice, but it was the only choice that I believed was available to me. Here I was, a twenty-three-year-old woman. I hadn't even been out of high school long enough to be sent a ten-year high school reunion notice, but home still represented support—it was where I had someone in my corner. It felt that way to my spiritual self, and I was deeply hoping that the church would once again bring calm to the storm that was raging inside.

When I returned home, my mum welcomed me with open arms and a little dash of "I told you so." But Mum would also be the one to hold me up on those hard days when I struggled to stand. Mum made phone calls, and a plan was hatched. It was agreed that if I came to church, they would hold a special prayer for me after the service. I felt like I was going to tip over any moment, teetering on a mental and emotional break; every fibre of my being was on fire, I felt as though I was burning from the inside out. Battle worn, my defenses were down, and every dark thought had access to my mind. The voices, a constant barrage of criticism—I was told it was the Enemy's voice. I was scared, and I was scared for myself.

The mounting cognitive dissonance and the ongoing psychological stress heightened this experience. Having hands laid on me as the prayer warriors waged war for my soul caused my body to shake. "This is a sign that God is at work."

"The Enemy wants Susan, it's going to be a battle, but God will win in the end—that's what I'm hearing." "In the name of Jesus! I bind the Enemy at work, and I loose the power of the Holy Spirit over her." "I bind every dark force at work and loose angels on Susan's behalf." Prayer after prayer and prophecy after prophecy were spoken over me. I shook, I trembled, and I found myself crying out as the fervency of their prayers rose. I was beginning to believe that maybe I did pick up evil spirits after all—especially considering no one forced me to say yes to the seminars. "Please help me, God," I prayed.

Feeling supported and protected seemed to calm my brain for some time, at least, but as soon as I experienced another stressor, I began to spiral again. Receiving support, even though it came through prayer, gave me something to hold onto. For a moment, however brief, I truly believed that God was on my side, and that maybe, just maybe, there was a light at the end of this tunnel.

I was just shy of turning twenty-five and I pushed myself to the limit, using every resource I had. Yet, the more I tried, the more I fell short, and all I could see was that I was falling short. I noticed that what used to work was no longer working for me. And the more I tried, the less I was able to move forward. It was a small beginning, but a beginning nonetheless—I was starting to look inward and to self-resource, and at this point, the only resource I had was the church.

When I called the church to speak with someone, I was referred to a woman named Judy. Judy was the wife of one of the pastors, and she was also a leader in the church. When we spoke over the phone, she responded with clarity and deep insight that resonated with me. That call was an easy hook. I was welcomed with a warm and friendly greeting as I entered the church. The front entry of the church foyer had clear glass that allowed the light to welcome everyone. Once inside, as I walked through the wood-paneled double doors into the sanctuary, I saw the familiar plush red carpet and velvet curtains—they seemed to welcome me. In some strange way, it felt as though I had come home. The sanctuary had some updated musical instruments to the side, and in the centre stood a wooden podium that commanded respect.

The Full Gospel Church became my new home, and I reconnected in every way I could. Judy led the singles group. Even though I could have joined the young adults, I found myself bonding with the middle-aged, forever single women and the divorcees. They welcomed me with open arms; my presence seemed to add a youthfulness and vitality to the group. They offered me their insights on life and the Lord's ways. At their recommendation, I read the books they liked, attempted to connect with a few young adults my age, cut my hair, and changed the way I dressed. I mirrored my surroundings and I became one of them. But, my inner critic remained. Ultimately, this voice became so loud that it drowned out every other voice.

Getting reconnected to a church that had a building with four walls rather than a house church was enough of a difference to make it seem new. There weren't those sparks of similarity to elicit intrusive thoughts from my childhood. The Full Gospel Church wasn't a living room—it was a sanctuary alive with sound. Multiple instruments and a worship team led by a worship leader carried the congregation, turning simple songs into living experiences. There was still just enough pause in the music for a prophetic utterance and speaking in tongues, but because many of the people in the pews were doing it, it felt less threatening. My mind didn't clock it as a similar threat.

I spent my first year in the church becoming enmeshed, just as I did in the last group I attached myself to. I went to every service, every Bible study, every singles dinner, and when a new opportunity came knocking at my door, I gladly grabbed the handle and swung my life wide open! "Thank you, I'd love too!" "You need help?" "Yes, I can do that!" "Stay longer? No problem." "You need someone to volunteer for the Christmas dinner we're hosting for the homeless? I'm you're girl!" It was that kind of connection.

And then, I did something I didn't think I'd ever do … I cut off my hair! I wanted to leave my old life behind, so what better way than a new haircut? It was the year that the beloved Julia Roberts—yes, the movie actress—cut off her gorgeous ruby red locs for a fabulous short cut. When I went to see my hairstylist one day, Julia was on the front cover of a celebrity hairstyle magazine with her short hair, so I gave him the magazine and said, "Yes! Let's do that." When I returned to church, it was interesting to see everyone's reaction. Remember, it was still the year of big hair and shoulder pads. In everything that I was doing to create that sense of belonging, once the initial newness wore off and all the excitement that comes with "new," I would find this sense of ache relodging itself right behind my heart, knocking and leaving what felt like large bruises each time it did. I kept myself busy with volunteering, shopping, reading the latest book handed to me, and going to singles and young adult meetings to keep my chin up.

Then, one day at a young adults meeting, I was standing to the side in the sanctuary waiting for worship to start and

I found myself watching everyone talking and laughing as they did the Christian boy-girl things they do. In that instant, I realized that despite all my effort, I wasn't one of them and I never would be. That thought became a slippery slope. Feeling threatened from noticing I was not fitting in, my brain began to slide down that slope and focus only on the fact that I was welcome … but only to the edge of the room, or only to the limit of their comfort.

I have often wondered which self was trying to take centre stage at this point on my journey. I could never tell if it was my normal self wanting the ability to set goals and achieve, even if that goal was to belong, or if it was my spiritual self finally connecting more dots only to be bombarded by more cognitive dissonance. I didn't know how to fit in, how to belong, if the church was right after all about me being a sinner in need of a Saviour. *How am I suppose to love this God who hates me? Do I really feel God's presence or is it just a normal sensation of social cohesion when I see others nodding their heads?* Feeling overwhelmed again, I sought out a previous source of comfort and strength and … I hatched an escape plan.

December 11th, 1989—D-Day for me. I took part in the church's Christmas concert. As I stood on the lush red-carpeted stage, claiming my spot as one of the choir members, I found myself repeating lines that no longer connected to my heart. My escape plan was set in motion, as I had decided to return to my LGAT family and to the man twenty-five years my senior as soon as the concert ended. I invited my LGAT family to the Christmas concert and they did not disappoint me; that magical mix I used to call my family literally took up the first two rows on the right-hand side of the church. It was obvious that no one explained to them church formality;

they sat front and centre to show me how much I meant to them, even after months apart.

But the plan I hatched was not meant to be. After the concert, I was rejected. It stopped me in my tracks. "I can't take you back, Susan, you've changed. Watching you up on the stage tonight, dressed how you're dressed, you're not the person I thought you were; so, no, I can't take you back," he said. Those words stung. "What do you mean you won't take me back? You couldn't get enough of me a few months ago. You literally begged me not to leave our relationship," I pleaded. And when I stepped out of his car that night, I stepped out of myself. My spiritual self couldn't get it right either. *What am I doing with my life?* Nothing made sense.

When I got back to my shared apartment, I went into the bathroom and fell to my knees—the floor caught any strength I had left. I was in agony. Attempting to steer my thoughts towards positive memories like my love for my niece and nephew fell short. Prayer seemed powerless. I was stripped of strength; my bones were weary from trying so hard to fit in. I was drowning in emotion. I felt as though I was being swallowed up by darkness. I cried until silence took over. I couldn't find the strength to pray anymore. When I opened my eyes, I was somewhere in between—not here or there, not wanted or loved. It felt like I was caught in a constant dance between trying to fit in and trying to belong. Fitting in was like forcing my feet into shoes that were two sizes too small—painful, but familiar. Belonging, though, came with its own cost; it felt like I could never say no without risking everything.

That push and pull created its own kind of bond—not love, but survival—and I learned to move with tight steps and a yes on my lips. Chasing information, trying to follow the steps I didn't quite fully learn then suddenly they would change, and it would leave me chasing and trying again, and again, and again. Getting so close, but never quite reaching the finish line. My mind became the battleground. Questioning everything, every move, trying to predict the unpredictable, I felt stuck, and I wanted the pain to stop.

The morning after the concert, I would attempt to end my pain; I would self-destruct and self-harm. I believe that what stopped me, more than the image of any family missing me or the knowledge that I was letting people down, was *fear*: fear of going to Hell, fear of facing God, fear of what was waiting for me on the other side. I caused enough self-harm that I would need medical intervention.

I picked up the phone and called Judy. Judy had become my safe place and my go-to person over the last few months. "Hi, Judy? It's Susan, I've done something stupid, and I think I need help." Judy quickly sent help. Judy's husband, Pastor Dan, and the youth pastor came to rescue me. Together, they took me to Judy so she could assess my situation. Judy had a previous background in nursing and when she saw me, I shared everything. There was no time wasted. It would be Judy who would advocate for me at the hospital. Judy was at my bedside as they pumped my stomach, and it would be Judy who would speak on my behalf when I showed them my wounds. After medical treatment, I was sent to another hospital where I was psychologically assessed. I was put into an interview room behind a one-way glass window. As I waited, the reality and the enormity of recent events landed: *Oh shit, Susan, what have you done now!? Now what's going to happen!* I was scared. I was scared for my well-being and scared for my future.

So, I did what I was primed to do: I prayed. I prayed with everything in me, asking God to help me. "God, I can't do this anymore. I give my life to you, Lord Jesus. I'm a mess and I can't get anything right. Take my life, I don't want it anymore. Jesus, I ask you to come into my heart. Please help me, I'm yours. In Jesus's name." It was more a prayer of giving away than asking. When I said that prayer, nothing monumental happened—no signs or special effects—but I do remember wondering if there was anyone on the other side of the one-way glass watching me. *It doesn't matter*, I thought to myself. I knew what I wanted, and I wanted this. This time, when I said the Sinner's prayer, no one had to tell me to give my life—I freely gave it away.

Actually, that was a fear response, but that's for later.

Time passed, a doctor came into the room and talked to me. After a few quick questions, he left saying he would be back shortly. By this time, Judy was allowed to come and join me in the room, and as we waited for the doctor to return, I shared with Judy that I asked Jesus into my heart again, but Judy still thought it was best if we prayed together, sealing the deal; then she knew that I knew I had given my life to Christ.

The doctor informed Judy and I about the next steps, and it turned out we had a choice to make. There was a bed available in the psychiatric ward, or, if I had twenty-four-hour care, they would release me into my pastor's care until I could meet with the psychiatrist, which was to be within the next few days. With a family history of having to visit a psychiatric hospital to see my grandmother, I looked at Judy and asked her to pick option two. "As long as you promise to not do anything more, I will let you come home with me," Judy said. "I promise." It was so easy to say. "Okay," Judy said, as she faced the doctor, "we will take Susan home with us and someone will be with her twenty-four seven."

See, this time I did really get saved! My prayers were already being answered.

Threads I hold,

Where do I start? Susan, I still find myself taking time to find words to articulate what it was like to be a twenty-four year old with her mind and body disassociated as you tried to keep your life afloat in an ocean of unresolved emotions, fears, struggles, disappointments, minimized trauma, and lack of support. From exhausting your under-resourced self to trying everything you know to fit and belong. Whew! That's a lot. Let's take a deep breath, let it out slowly. Okay, let's take another breath and let it out slowly, whew!

I'm so grateful you will get to tell your story and that you finally believe that your story matters, it definitely matters to me. I'm grateful that you got the physical care that you needed and I still wonder what might have happened if you had chosen option one and gone into the psychiatric unit, where medical care might have happened from a scientific perspective rather than a religious perspective. Would you have received the psychological care that would begin to undo the religious influence in your life? Would you have received the care to undo the harm done to your brain in the personal development program? Or would you have entered a medical system that was unaware of the profound effects of undue influence, coercive control, or religious and spiritual trauma? After all, it was still the late 80s and you are sensitive to your environment.

Choosing door number two seemed so right for so many reasons. There is a new term today that is yet to go into the DSM-5 (Diagnostic and Statistical Manual of Mental Disorders) as a diagnosis. C-PTSD is caused by long-term abuse or trauma in which the individual perceives little or no chance of escape (helplessness). Still today, you have never had an official diagnosis, but we both know then and now that your body has been keeping score.

Susan, what you will receive at this stage of your life will be two things that will make a big difference. First, you will be put on medicine that can be helpful in treating major depressive episodes and PTSD. This medicine will give your brain the emotional reprieve it desperately needs. Second, social support, real human beings who surround you and support you twenty-four seven. I would also like to say that this is also a yellow flag that will quickly turn red because the vulnerabilities in your life, especially your need for connection and belonging, still leave you open and at risk. Where you find this support will influence— unduly—your life choices. Belonging is very much a part of the human experience and it's part of what humans need in order to thrive, yet when belonging comes from a void, it is already a vulnerability. And when it is mixed with intensity, pleasure, and pain, it creates a bond like Velcro. I call it Velcro Kisses. Get ready.

Trauma is a fact of life. It does not, however, have to be a life sentence.

—Peter Levine

9

I BELONG

Judy was my hero and my new source of connection. If Judy left the house for any reason whatsoever, someone would be at my side. It was the first time I felt cared for and supported going through something difficult, rather than having to survive the situation on my own. I felt like a family member while I lived with Judy and her real family. For the next eight weeks, they watched over me and gave me time and space to unthaw, reconnect, and recalibrate to my new stance in life. It was a new feeling being resourced in this way. Having people support me, surround me, and be there to go through something with me was a powerful experience and I became a sponge soaking up every drop.

The psychiatrist that I was to meet would become my psychiatrist for the next five years. Dr. Reed was the head of psychiatry at the Calgary General Hospital, and after meeting with me, he agreed to take me on as his patient. In the beginning, we met weekly. "Okay, I see that you have had a lot to deal with. I wonder why you haven't talked about your childhood trauma. You have all the symptoms that tell me something's happened to you. Do you want to talk about that a little?" "Wow, no one's ever asked me that!" my face turned bright red. "I know things have happened, but I just didn't think about them as childhood trauma. And I don't want my parents to get mad at me. I don't think anyone would really believe me if I shared everything, anyway." For the first time, I felt as though someone important actually cared. Yes, Judy cared, but this was a doctor, and he didn't want anything from me. "I'll share some things with you, but I need time. This is a lot and I'm still getting used to the medicine you've given me." Dr. Reed responded, "Yes, I know we spoke over the phone during the holidays, how are you feeling on the meds now?" "Better than last week, I can actually go out to the store with Judy now," I shared.

I can remember thinking that Dr. Reed was the first medical doctor to ever ask me if I had ever experienced childhood trauma because of the symptoms he saw in me. I listened intently as he gave explanations and definitions for what I had been through. Dr. Reed was the first qualified individual who worked with me as I began to process some of my childhood traumas—I had never thought in terms of trauma before. To me, it was just my life. One session, Dr. Reed suggested an idea, "What if you asked your parents to come to a session and share with them anything you want to about your childhood?" I couldn't grasp the idea. Sharing with Dr. Reed was something I could handle, but I wasn't sure about my parents. "Would they believe me? I think they would be angry with me and then what would happen?" I said as panic began to swell within my chest. Dr. Reed answered my questions but there were so many unknowns which only increased my anxiety. But Dr. Reed made a way. He made space and had the expertise to help me define and share what happened to me. Dr. Reed literally sat in the middle of the room and sheltered me as I, as a twenty-five-year-old young woman, for the first time in my life, gave voice to some of my trauma. It was a beginning, a great beginning.

My spiritual self was about to intercept and derail my healing by way of water. I received a prescription for a new medication from the hospital, but my mounting anxiety that led to panic attacks whenever I left Judy's home made me believe that maybe it was spiritual in nature after all. Each Sunday, we would need to arrive at church early because they were pastors, and even the car ride on the way to the service became a prayer meeting. I remember asking, "Who do I pray to: Father God, Jesus, or the Holy Spirit?" The names seemed to be intertwined. When I watched altar calls at church, "in Jesus's name" would often be followed by sending away some evil spirit, or the Holy Spirit would be asked for insight, almost as if it has directions no one else knew. God would be mentioned in prayer as Father God, somewhat like sitting around a table with Father God sitting at the end. My reason for asking for water baptism was that if I had anything left over, attached to me from my old self, I wanted it gone. Then, maybe all my troubling thoughts would be washed away too, especially the ache. That ache left me as soon as I was taken into Judy's home, but it would sneak up on me whenever she was out of my sight and bite me as a reminder that I was still alone.

When I came up from underneath the water that evening, I truly believed that I had been renewed like it talks about in 2 Corinthians 5:17, "old things had passed away; behold, all things have become new." The old Susan was "dead in Christ," and now, not only had my sins been washed away, but I believed my past was erased clean too. I had a blank slate and that equaled new beginnings.

So new in fact, that, still wet, Judy and I went into the pastoral office and she prayed for me to receive the baptism of the Holy Spirit, and one utterance came out of me, "Shunda le unda," I heard that before. "Shunda le unda," I said it again. "Wow, that was fast," said Judy. "Have you been prayed over before?" "No," which was a white lie. I didn't want to lose face in front of Judy, but someone had prayed for the baptism of the Holy Spirit before—Jenny in my teens. A voice inside me asked me why I thought I would be disappointing Judy if I told her the truth. I ignored it. "Okay, well, just keep practising with what the Holy Spirit is giving you and your prayer language will increase." Judy said as she shifted her weight to lift herself from the carpet. As I found my feet, I stood and recognized a gentle warmth inside me. I felt loved and I felt like I was where I was meant to be.

About a month into my stay with Judy and her family, there was such an improvement in my mental health that they felt it was time to branch out on my own. My new church community paid for six months of rent at an apartment that Judy and I had found. My new apartment was on the main floor in a quiet building just outside of the downtown core, still enabling me to walk to work. Yes, I was now working again. My father had made some phone calls, and I was offered a position at the company headquarters where he worked. With my weekly appointments with Dr. Reed, Judy keeping an eye on me, and now getting back into the workforce, I felt like my self-harm situation was just a bump in the road. *Silly me for trying to get attention by self-harming. Whose attention was I trying to get?* Except it wasn't just a bump—it was very real, and I had yet to discover just how real it was.

I knew the value of hard work and with the help of my father, I was back at work within weeks. I believed for the first time in a long time that God was pleased with me, and that was my proof. No one explained to me back then that when support is given in these ways, it fosters bonding, connection, and the ability to heal. Because of these new experiences and my belief that my past was gone, I stopped sharing as much in therapy, and if I did, I talked about God. It was about how different I felt, and how happy I was. Dr. Reed commented on how fast I made progress and how it seemed that my new faith and my belief in God gave me an unexpectedly fast recovery. However, he still wanted me to keep my appointments, and thank God he did—in time, I would come to see just how much Dr. Reed was exactly what I needed.

Within six months, I accomplished a lot: I was living and working on my own, going to church, and deeply connecting with my new community. I was a living testimony to the power of God. People at church talked about my testimony and I did not want to disappoint. Yet, what people didn't see was how dependent I was on an outside source of approval. I relied on receiving approval from Judy, the church, and my community. I would show up to every meeting, every Sunday service, and every time I was asked to help, I said yes. My sense of self was mixed with my performance. My self was being formed from the outside in rather than from the inside out. This was my new Christian life.

Threads I hold,
Oh, Susan, you have been hoodwinked, dupped, and you
don't even know it. I wish I could swoop in and rescue you
and show you just how damaging this all is. Yet, support
and the bonds of belonging will hook you many times over

into doing what you think you should, i.e., what the environment determines to be the shoulds and should-nots. The list is long; it will change many times, and you will change with it. You don't know this as a form of behaviour control; you just feel the fear of disapproval. What you've been taught is that fear is not of God, so fear, therefore, must be bad. Again, red flag. I can see how you might feel a sense of security, even stability, but it's conditional. You are being primed to become a people pleaser, and you become an expert people pleaser. I know you're hooked by wanting to fit in and belong somewhere, yet, because there are many generational families within the same church, you will continue to be plagued by feeling that you are still an outsider no matter how hard you try. By the sheer fact of relational numbers, you are outnumbered. I understand the power it has over you, the deep desire to have a place, to be part of a community, to find your tribe—a place where everyone belongs and where everyone looks out for one another. Such an idyllic picture. But it's not here. Utopia is not here.

Don't get me wrong, Susan, I know how over the years you will come to experience that powerful force of belonging, connection, and community, and living according to those forces makes you feel like you're flourishing. You will come to believe, more than once, that you've found "your people" and you will give your all many times. There are many things I wish I could warn you about, especially what it's like for a woman in these environments and systems. The vulnerabilities that you have are a perfect fit, complementing the system flawlessly, adding to its enticement. You are entering a system where doctrine is valued more than people, where critical thought is discouraged, and where submission and authority take on entirely new meanings. You will be discouraged from creating your own internal locus of control; in its place, you will be taught submission in many forms. You will be taught lessons about a woman's role, both spoken and unspoken, until you meet a network that endorses women, powerful women. It will be here in this new network, the New Apostolic network, that it's going to be a wild ride.

Trauma causes people to remain stuck in interpreting the present in light of an unchanging past.

—Bessel van der Kolk

10

INDOCTRINATION

Seeing as I was new to church history and theology, I came to learn that each church I attended had some form of doctrinal difference; some had different degrees of emphasis regarding certain elements of doctrine, while others had entirely different worldviews. For instance, Full Gospel Church was a Pentecostal church. Pentecostals, like all charismatic churches, believe in both the baptism of the Holy Spirit and in baptism by water, the combination of which enables a Christian to live a Spirit-filled and empowered life. What distinguishes Pentecostals from other charismatic forms of Christianity is the belief that the baptism of the Holy Spirit is evidenced only by speaking in tongues.

During my time at Full Gospel Church, there was another large influence within charismatic churches: spiritual outpourings called revivals, the most notable of which include the Toronto Blessing (1994, Toronto Airport Vineyard) and the Brownsville Revival (1995, Pensacola, Florida). Church members who had experienced the Toronto Blessing returned believing that it was your right as a believer to have an awakening, which was a personal experience of God's presence and power. This brought criticism primarily centred around disagreements about charismatic doctrine, the Latter Rain Movement, and whether or not the physical manifestations people experienced were in line with biblical doctrine. The

Toronto Blessing would become synonymous within charismatic Christian circles with an increased awareness of God's love, religious ecstasy, external observances of ecstatic worship, being slain in the Spirit, uncontrollable laughter, emotional and/or physical euphoria, crying, healing from emotional wounds, healing from damaged relationships, and electric waves of the Spirit. Holy laughter as a result of overwhelming joy was a hallmark manifestation and there were also some reports of participants roaring like lions or making other animal noises.

I met my first husband while I was attending Full Gospel Church, which happened to be heavily influenced by the Toronto Blessing. This move of God would cause a division in our church. On the one side were the "on fire" people, and on the other side was what I call "the Word" people. It was evident who was on which side. Almost every person who made the journey to experience the Toronto Blessing came back visibly changed. I would only get the chance to join one service later in the 90s, but I heard many stories from the beginning. Our church had manifestations like speaking in tongues and prophecy within context, but these people came back on fire and hungry for more of what they had experienced at the Toronto Airport church. It reminded me of when I first saw Iris after she'd been through the personal development course. Those who had this new experience described God as their Father, speaking about the love of God; while those on the other side of the line anchored themselves in God's Word and the foundational beliefs of sin, repentance, and salvation. A diversity of opinions were obvious between the two sides and after a time, the pressure created a fracture and the church split over the emphasis of experience-over-the-Word versus the-Word-over-experience.

I was still a young believer at the time and did not have an understanding of outpourings, moves of God, or the new things God was doing. When I was asked my opinion about receiving visions and the experiential way people were having encounters with God, I trusted people when they said they had an experience. But I wasn't ready for the betrayal that came as my name, information, and opinion were weaponized and used against people that I cared about—those who had helped me the most: Judy and her family. It was as though I was a chess piece that was just sacrificed to make someone else's plan work.

The congregation voted with their feet; many walked away, and some members of the leadership team branched off and started their own ministries. My insides were screaming. I felt as though I had just been used for someone else's agenda. I tried to focus on my upcoming wedding, but this gnawing would return every time I saw a wedding invitation decline. First from the head pastor, then from Judy and her family—many of our closest friends would decline our invitations.

John Henry and I were married on the shortest day of the year: December 21, 1991. For our wedding ceremony, we had not one but two pastors. One pastor gave the salvation message while the other pastor spoke on God's love and grace. Geesh! How even in this "new life," my worlds were still split in two. Once we were married, John Henry and I thought that this would be an opportunity to find a new church that we could call home as a newly married couple.

Maybe it was getting married and checking off that box that triggered my subconscious patterns, but upon returning to Calgary after our honeymoon, John Henry and I put in the video tapes and watched the original *Left Behind*.

We watched as the Rapture occurred without warning! In an instant, millions of people, including children, vanished, leaving behind empty clothes, crashed cars, and chaos. Those who remained were overwhelmed with confusion, panic, and grief. Many struggled to comprehend what happened. Some even assume mass kidnappings, alien abductions, or a global conspiracy, until a few lucky ones (maybe even those who had praying mothers) began to wake up and realize the truth: The Christians didn't vanish, they were raptured—taken to Heaven. It would seem that I should be realizing that what I was told as a young girl, and what I had subconsciously tucked away in the back of my mind, was now being played out on the television screen before me. But I didn't. I was disconnected. John Henry also believed that the Rapture would happen, but I do not recall us openly discussing the Rapture other than knowing that there would be, as my mum would put it, "signs of the times." My next thought was, *Well, at least I got to get married before Jesus returned.*

Seeing as I was married in the early 90s and primed to mirror my environment, I found myself becoming increasingly invested in the fear mongering known as the Satanic panic, which began to gain a foothold in certain churches and in North America in general. The *Left Behind* movies would be replaced with books about the Satanic panic about how Satan was taking over our children, our schools, and our world. As I absorbed each book, each video, each teaching, my mind weaved together striking scenes and vivid pictures exposing how dark this world was becoming. I consumed information from Tex Mars, Mike Warnke, and Rebecca Brown as the TV documented allegations of satanic ritual abuse and conspiracy theories. There were conspiracies of satanic involvement in everything from the government to music. No child was safe, even the Care Bears and Teletubbies were being used by the Enemy. Evil was all around us!

God said ...

—The Bible

11

THE NEW APOSTOLIC REFORMATION

It wasn't long after leaving Full Gospel Church that John Henry and I ended up looking for a new church to join. John Henry was invited to a men's breakfast where he heard a man speak about the fathers and mothers in the faith. When he came back, I could see that something was different. He told me about how this men's breakfast was not only a meal, but a ministry. We decided to seek this speaker out, and it just so happened that he was an intern pastor at a Mennonite church. But this wasn't just any Mennonite church; this church was open to all that God had for His people and that included learning to prophetically hear God speak to us personally. That grabbed our attention, and we didn't let go—clearly a Velcro Kiss.

Pineridge Christian Fellowship belonged to the Calgary Mennonite Fellowship and was on the "cutting edge" of theology, where the pastor would not only call himself a prophet of God, but would teach those of us who attended his church how to hear God for ourselves. Prophecy and hearing God was taught in churches that were associated with the New Apostolic Reformation (NAR). The NAR is considered more of a network rather than a specific affiliation or formal denomination. This shifts the focus from institutional structures to relational connections, from walls to webs or networks that emphasize relationship, collaboration, and shared movement.

A move from a denomination that builds fences, to define who's in and who's out, to a network that builds connections that reach everywhere. Many of the prominent leaders in the NAR were influenced by the Toronto Blessing, so its members often advocated for many of the same theological points: prophecy, spiritual warfare, apostles, prophets, the supernatural lifestyle, and eventually the Seven Mountain Mandate. Even though Mennonite churches aren't typically associated with these charismatic theologies, Pineridge was becoming increasingly enmeshed with important people within the NAR network, and there were enough prophetic elements at this Mennonite church to keep John Henry and I hooked. It served as a launch pad for our connection to other churches that were even more affiliated with the New Apostolic Reformation.

Within these churches, I experienced the draw of the prophetic which quickly became an addiction—something I didn't recognize at first, but soon couldn't seem to live without. It started innocently enough. The desire and draw of wanting to hear God. Coming out of a difficult season, the need for direction and stability was a strong pull. My husband and I were in search of direction and a sense of meaning. Throughout this season, I was working at an exploration company in downtown Calgary—I was advancing in the company, I was making new friends, joining clubs, yet even with this forward movement in my life, underneath it all, I continued to carry anxiety as an unshakable presence in my life.

And this anxiety has a name: Rapture anxiety. It would come up at the oddest times. At work, this anxiety would show up when my coworkers would talk about their future plans—from purchasing their first home, to vacations, even planning a family. My mind would get triggered, stuck in a loop, constantly wondering why my life never seemed to move forward. Since getting married, within a year, we had moved three times, and all the moving only left me with more questions. As I compared my life to others, I often felt behind the curve. Instead of working towards purchasing a home, we were living paycheck to paycheck. My husband changed jobs often, which left me as our main source of steady income. Rapture anxiety showed up feeling as though I didn't quite fit into life; somehow, it was as though I was "out of step" with the rhythms of normal life. That feeling of not quite fitting in primed me, so when I found myself connecting to someone who actually heard God, knew God's thoughts, and saw what was coming in the future, I was immediately hooked—no questions asked. Apostles, prophets, and eventually the supernatural lifestyle would now become my lifeline.

Church history was a maze on its own, and theology is a whole other puzzle I'm not sure I'm fully able to piece together. But, I did quickly become enamored by the prophets of the NAR. I likened these prophets to some kind of meta-humans—those who had powers beyond this natural realm. Prophets were the keepers of the unseen and mystical realms and were God's chosen and appointed. They and they alone were given both the permission and authority to wield the ancient powers of God. Prophets were appointed by God "over the nations and over the kingdoms, to root out and to pull down, to destroy and to throw down, to build and to plant" (Jeremiah 1:10). It's all part of God's mandate to bring the Kingdom of Heaven to Earth. It's heady, it's heavy, and it can also be scary. Especially when you're found on the "wrong" side.

When I first experienced a prophetic word, it felt as though I just encountered a superpowered individual who just knew things about me. It was as though they had access to my conversations, emails, Facebook, and Instagram accounts. They somehow knew about some of the most intimate details of my life—even my dream states weren't secret anymore. Prophets could pinpoint who you were and what you were feeling. They had divine knowledge about circumstances and situations that you were in, and they told you God's way through it all—creating breakthrough after breakthrough.

Breakthrough in the context of prophecy in the NAR is often understood as a decisive moment when spiritual barriers are overcome and God's power is manifested in a new way. Whether that is overcoming personal struggles, demonic opposition, or roadblocks in one's life, breakthrough allows one to step into a new level of freedom, blessing, and influence. Breakthrough is frequently contextually connected to spiritual warfare, where there is an emphasis on prayer, fasting, prophetic declarations, or decrees that would create shifts in the spiritual atmosphere so that God's Kingdom purposes could be advanced. Breakthrough can be both personal and collective, especially as it is often linked to the idea of advancing God's Kingdom in society and moving into a new season of influence or revival.

Having special revelatory insights and knowledge made the prophets powerful. My experiences in the prophetic realm were profound. When I had a prophecy spoken to me, called receiving a prophetic word, it had the ability to still my soul, shift direction, and reawaken my sense of purpose. I can attest when a prophet calls you out of a crowd of people, you feel as though Heaven sees you. You are wrapped in this energy that could only be described as the breath of Heaven. It shifts something inside of you; it's like oxygen to your soul. It was to mine.

Threads I hold,

*Susan, as this new indoctrination process takes over, your thoughts, behaviours, and emotions are being influenced without your awareness. This **will** change you. You will literally feel a new sense of self as you take on the roles of a prophetic intercessor—that of a prayer warrior for the Kingdom. You will learn to hear God's voice for yourself and then you will speak on God's behalf to others. You will go on to live your life following the prophetic words given by the apostles and the prophets in your sphere. You will become trauma bonded to the prophetic word and to prophecy. It will be as though you are bonded by Velcro to this movement. And that, my dear Susan, is where the cycle begins, the push-pull, on again-off again cycles. The love bombing, affection, attention, and praise will have you emotionally and financially invested until you find yourself on the outside, where you will be talked about and left spinning in confusion and second guessing keeps you hooked. You will try your hardest again and again until finally you will have had enough and begin the process of detaching yourself from this movement. It will turn out in your favour in the end.*

Prophecy: an inspired utterance of a prophet, the function or vocation of a prophet specifically the inspired declaration of divine will and purpose, a prediction of something to come.

—Merriam-Webster's Dictionary

PROPHECY

My first powerful experience of prophecy was at a women's conference in Edmonton. I left my two young children with my sister and took advantage of the opportunity to experience my first women's conference. In the NAR, there are female prophets who are called prophetesses and at this women's meeting, the prophetess was well-known. Her words shifted the atmosphere—count me in! As I walked into the conference, I could feel something in the air: It was expectation, thick and electric. As each of us took our seats, I could feel my heart beating with anticipation. When Claire Hunter entered the room, everything shifted. As soon as I laid eyes on her, I was mesmerized—Claire belonged in this room, and she belonged to someone bigger than this room. I felt as though I had been waiting all my life for her to arrive.

Claire Hunter was an internationally known prophetess and the daughter-in-law of a man who established an entire ministry within the NAR. That ministry provided prophetic training and specialized in the restoration of the church and what to expect next on God's agenda. Claire was beautiful and her dress was impeccable; it was as though she almost didn't need to say anything as her strength and confidence permeated the air. I needed Claire to prophesy over me.

Throughout the weekend, I watched as Claire gave powerful prophetic words. She could see straight into your circumstances and her words carried the weight of Heaven. It was as though you knew God had your number, and He was calling you directly—through Claire. As Claire prophesied, individuals were visibly moved as the words that were spoken shifted something inside them. I watched as people shook as though something was running through their bodies; they struggled to stay grounded, finally surrendering to the power as they fell to the floor, ushers' hands ready to catch them as they fell under the power of the Holy Spirit.

As I took my place in the prayer line, I could feel Claire's presence close to me, yet her voice felt distant. I opened my eyes, turning my head to follow her voice. Claire was still rows away from me. *Wow, she does carry a powerful anointing.* I faced forward and closed my eyes, soaking in the music and anticipating my turn. By the time it was my turn to be prayed for, another minister stepped in and prayed for me, as it took many ministers to cover the sheer number of women wanting prayer.

Claire had spent much of the conference discussing new revelations and ended each session with a prophetic prayer, prophecy, or impartation. In one meeting, when there was intercession for marriages, I found myself bent over, unable to straighten up. It felt as though someone had their hand pressed on my back, holding me down, keeping me from standing up straight. There was a tangible energy to this experience. This was the first time anything supernatural like this happened to me and when the whole experience was over, I knew I wanted more—another Velcro Kiss.

When the final night of the conference arrived, I found myself secretly asking God to have Claire prophesy over me. My heart sank when Claire set the tone for the evening saying that she would *not* be prophesying over individuals that night, but that God wanted her to do an impartation. An impartation is different from a prophecy in that a prophecy is often a direct and personal word from God spoken over a person, whereas an impartation is still from God, but it is usually done by the laying on of hands or by blowing lightly upon someone as they receive what Heaven releases.

As ministry time came, it was my turn—I was among a group—and we walked up onto the stage and turned to face the audience. When Claire came to where I was standing, she stopped, and rather than placing her hands on my shoulders and moving onto the next person, I heard her say as she stood in front of me, "Okay, Lord," and then the unbelievable happened—Claire began to prophesy over me! Definitely a Velcro Kiss.

Immediately, my body felt heat and electricity as wave after wave of thick energy rose up inside of me, at the same time, energy swirled around me. The experience was undeniable, I had seen other's doing what I was now doing: groaning, shaking, and bending over. I didn't fall, but I knew something just happened—I was sure of it. The experience only took a minute or two. The prophetic word that Claire spoke over my life that night announced to me, and in my mind, that God was giving me a breaker anointing. She spoke that I was going to need to "rise up" into this anointing that God was placing inside of me. Claire prophesied:

The Lord would say, daughter, don't be surprised that you will walk through many things, things that will seem dire, that will seem desperate but know that God is using all this as training. God wants you to "rise up" into the anointing that He has placed on the inside of you. Now, Lord, I declare breakthrough on every side. Thank you, Lord, for this word.

It was more than a kiss from Heaven; this raw and priming moment would be remembered forever. This was a Kiss that bonded me to the prophetic movement. I was hooked. When I used to listen to the tape recording, I could hear myself through Claire's words and as she spoke, I remember hearing the sounds that came out of my mouth, sounds raw and primal, as if I was birthing something unseen. This word was life. In the coming years, I would declare this word out loud anytime I encountered a situation or circumstance that seemed dire or desperate. I would hold fast to this prophetic word as I looked for God's breakthrough.

From that night forward, my life was changed. From that night forward, I began to look at life differently. I believed God knew my name, that He knew who I was. From that night forward, I believed I had a special purpose for my life, and everything I had experienced up until that point all seemed to make sense to me now. It was all "just training." All those difficult and traumatic things that happened in my life were "just training," and now that I had this knowledge, I would be able to breakthrough much sooner than I could have hoped. *Break* and *through*: Who knew that putting those two words together would hold so much power over me? Yet another Velcro Kiss.

Threads I hold,

Hook, Line, and Sinker could be the title of this experience. Wow! I'll start by taking a deep breath. Whew! The power of energetics and the dynamics between people can be astounding. People coming together creates a collective energy, and when that energy is focused, it exponentially produces a power all its own where things happen: where miracles can happen and where energies create attachments. I've learned from your experience, Susan; the longer you are involved, the more conferences and gatherings you go to, these energy systems and the supernatural experiences that you are experiencing will Velcro to you and affect your entire life. It won't be until you begin to unhook yourself by creating distance between you and these environments that you will learn just how contagious emotions are and how empathic individuals sense the emotional overtone of the room—they feel it before they can rationalize it.

Relational dynamics are energy dynamics, and you will learn about the influence of priming. Everything is influenced. In the NAR, you will have so many experiences that your brain learns to readily enter trance states and new states of being. From soaking sessions in worship, to extended prayer and prophecy times, to creating meditative states—you will come to crave these experiences. "You're addicted to the anointing," people say with a chuckle, laughing softly as though this is a good addiction to have. Just as an addict, Susan, you too will feel the withdrawal effects. You will come to learn about confirmation bias, where the brain begins to seek, interpret, and remember patterns that reinforce what we believe. It looks for confirming information as signs. But you are here now, at the beginning, and what you don't know, you don't know; so, I ask you to be kind to yourself as you deconstruct this foundation in your life. You just received your first prophecy, your first prophetic Velcro Kiss. And just like a passionate kiss, it made you heady, it was energizing, it was lifechanging, and it left you wanting more, much, much more. This will encourage an all-or-nothing mentality, but here you are in 2001. Here's two more words: Roller and Coaster.

Sometimes a breakthrough comes after the biggest breakdown of your life. Hang in there.

—The Mind

HEARING GOD

It was as if the church became the Sun and I was the Earth, circling around and around as the church became my source of life. The gravitational pull of community and likeminded friendships took root in my life—relationships that provided stability. I finally found what I had been looking for: acceptance in a community, which was the desire of my normal self, and the deep need for spiritual security, which was what my spiritual self desperately sought. I felt a profound joy that made it feel as though every hope I'd ever carried had finally come true.

Learning how to prophetically hear God took practice. Practising hearing God in the small things in life built my confidence as I began to see signs and confirmations everywhere. Practice came in different forms. For example, I would ask God about what colour I should choose each Sunday—it became almost a game to see who showed up in what colour. Colours were symbolic, i.e., if most of the people showed up in shades of blue, then, prophetically, that could signify that God was releasing His revelation that day. The colour blue, as all colours, had a positive sense and negative sense; in a positive sense, blue communicates communion or revelation, and in a negative sense, it could represent depression, sorrow, or anxiety.

Then, there was the practice of the *rhema* word. A *rhema* word is a deeply personal, timely, and a specific word of revelation that is illuminated by the Holy Spirit through Scripture. It is considered to be an alive and active word to a specific question. For example, I would ask God a question about the business that John Henry and I started, and as I read Scripture, a specific word or verse would leap off the pages and resonate deeply in my spirit. The passage might provide a clear direction, the path to take when we were making big decisions. God's *rhema* word became very important to me. Believing that God spoke this way opened a door of possibilities, allowing me to assign meaning to literally anything. Everything was now open territory with the *rhema* word charting the course. Claire shared in one of her messages that "God is always speaking, it is us who need to adjust our frequency so that we can be on the same frequency as God. We must fine-tune our spirits like a radio dial, trusting that with practice, we can hear God, for as His sons and daughters, nothing is hidden from us, and I pray for eyes to see and ears to hear your Spirit speaking to the Church today."

Practice, of course, came with courses and levels, each level building upon the last, deepening how to hear God. You know how much I love levels. We would practise each way that was imparted to us. Practice meant allowing our minds to be still to open our spiritual eyes to see. Often one word or a picture would come to me as I stood in front of my partner and as I gave that one word or that small picture, more would come to me. Words that painted a picture of where that person was in their life, even highlighting what they might be going through. Some images would be so clear and concise that it felt as though I was beginning to see another dimension.

Hearing God for others was intoxicating and powerful. Allowing myself to tune in to God's frequency, a frequency that felt as though it came from beyond ordinary understanding, beyond my own thoughts or imaginations, brought with it feelings that were personal, sacred, and powerful. These moments were supercharged with an unfamiliar intimacy that felt as though I was truly connecting with the third Heaven, as the Divine weaved messages into your soul. I can only describe these moments as an energetic bonding and resonance that changed both me and the person receiving the word. It's a Velcro Kiss that connects a person to this unseen realm and power that leaves you longing for more.

As I became more practiced, it was as though I put on new lenses, and I saw life in an entirely new way. I began to wonder if my spiritual self was actually my true self after all. I was all in.

Threads I hold,

Susan, I see that you are all in. You feel the power of energetic intimacy. Notice how you naturally overinvest yourself in every aspect of church and culture—from volunteering with the nursery to worship and back again to leadership. Meaning-making and thinking mystically has become your new template for life. It deceives you into believing that you now have a Magic 8 ball or "Heaven's insight" into everything! Every question now has an answer, even if that answer is simply "wait." You don't see it yet, but you are overemphasizing hearing God and applying what you hear to relational issues, business decisions, and everyday life. This will take its toll on you, but not yet;

it's giving you a lot of energy at this point in your story. Your bond to prophecy is growing stronger by the day. Time will tell.

Everything is energy and that's all there is to it.

—Albert Einstein

14

ON FIRE

I first experienced prophetic dance with flags when our family travelled to the United States on a business trip. We had become friends with a pastor from California and his family, as we would spend time together whenever they would travel to Calgary to minister at Pineridge. This set the stage for our developing friendship, especially between Rafe and my husband. When Rafe's wife accompanied him on his ministry trips, we spent time together as couples, sharing both conversation and friendship. On this trip to the US, Rafe, who was also a prophet, invited us to a church meeting. Attending any meeting with pastors or prophets meant exclusive access. This time, it came with second row seats, which happened to be behind the dancers. As worship began that night, the dancers moved and carried the Spirit's presence—they seemed to move to the rhythm of Heaven as they danced. As I watched the dancers, every step they took seemed to send electricity through my body. The dancers unraveled something deep within me as I gave my tears permission to speak for my heart. Something sacred took place that evening; I knew I wanted to see this happen at our church.

Returning to Canada, I scheduled a time to meet with our pastor and his wife to ask if I could create an opportunity for dance to be expressed at our church. I shared in detail what I both experienced and witnessed that evening with the dancers. Pastor Rowan took a moment, "Well, Susan, we'll pray about that and then let you know what God says." It was short, simple, and to the point. I submitted. *Well, at least they didn't say no*, I said to myself as I walked through the front door of the church. "God, I'm trusting you to bring dance into our church at the right time, I know dance is of you. You will birth dance here in our church. I mark today and I trust you, Lord. You ask me to submit to those in authority over my life and that you will take care of the details. I declare that dance will come to Pineridge, in Jesus's name." And with that, I trusted and obeyed.

However, after receiving Claire's prophecy and after returning home from the conference in Edmonton, I was "on fire," as they would say in Christianese. I had received a sign and I knew that trusting in the Lord and obeying His will had paid off. I was wholeheartedly engaged in what God was doing in my life. I returned with a renewed conviction to see a prophetic dance and flagging ministry exist at our church.

This time, when I went to my pastor, I went armed with a Scripture that I believed confirmed that it was God's timing to see dance released in our church. I felt as though this Scripture was the key that would open the door for dance to happen. A magical moment in my life.

Threads I hold,
Susan, it's true that you are having some amazing experiences. Experiences that allow you the ability to set goals, create momentum, build connections with others, and these things that you've experienced can naturally produce healing and a sense of well-being. Learning new

things, creativity, and bonded relationships are important in the human experience, and they are all factors of building resiliency—resiliency factors that you had in your life then lost. You will come to learn about attachment styles and their fundamental working in how we relate to others and connect to our environment. Learning about your attachment styles will be key in your future healing, one that you will learn in your fifties rather than in your twenties.

Connection is why we're here. We are hardwired to connect with others. It's what gives purpose and meaning to our lives, and without it there is suffering.

—Brené Brown

15

A DANCE MINISTRY AND A BUSINESS

Appointment Destiny became the official name of the dance ministry at our church. I believed the dance ministry's name came from none other than a *rhema* word from God, except this time, it came out of a book rather than Scripture. *Woman, Thou Art Loosed* by T.D. Jakes is based on Luke 13:12 where Jesus heals a woman who had been crippled for eighteen years and no one would help her, but Jesus called the woman to Him, on the Sabbath no less, and said to her "Woman, you are loosed from your infirmity." Jesus then lays His hands on her and she is immediately healed and glorifies God. T.D. Jakes's book spoke to women of the day, breaking the bonds in the world, as we too had "an appointment with destiny."

Appointment Destiny took form quickly and began to grow. Churches from our city began to connect with us, asking our team to impart prophetic dance in their churches. Our church also began to host more conferences with other prophetic names, and with each conference came the opportunity to minister in prophetic dance and flagging. Each dance would continue to embody God's voice through the medium of dance. Movement was woven into worship as approximately thirty dancers, both male and female, and importantly some Mennonite women would take part. Believing I was hearing God, I held the belief that anyone could be released in dance. I distinctly remember hearing these words in prayer, "If you get them to move from their hearts, they will release the anointing." And so, that's what I did. It seemed natural to me as I taught every dancer to move with the words, taking the words of the song and planting them deep in their hearts. This also meant that each dancer would spend time soaking in the music, repeating the song over and over.

When it came time to gather, we did so as a community. The church provided some of the finances, other items came from donations, and individuals who had owned businesses gave financially to put on these events. Some women in our church sewed our costumes, others helped with constructing props, while others provided support through prayer and intercession—a force as one rather than many. As each dancer entered the sanctuary, they held an elegant ballooned stemmed glass that held a small lit white candle with white chiffon swooped down from the bottom of the vase. The sanctuary lights were dimmed as the song began. I stood at the doorway, "Remember, this is for God, the people are just props." To another dancer, I said, "Remember, God knows you by name and He's so proud of you for doing this." Yet to another, "The anointing is all over you, you've got this; the people just get to watch." I encouraged each dancer as they entered the sanctuary. As I took my place in the dance that night, it felt as though generational weights were falling away as the women moved their bodies, souls, and spirits to the song.

With so many exciting things happening in our church community, I felt that I had reached a peak that my younger self could only dream of experiencing. As a family, we felt connected, supported, and valued as integral members of our church community. Opportunities to learn, to become established, to start our business, to lead the dance ministry, and the opportunity to be part of leadership were the ingredients that cemented us as members of this community.

Like Appointment Destiny, when we started our business, it came from prophetic words spoken over my husband. We received start up money from two of the prominent elders in our church, Andy and Bruce. I remember giving Andy, Bruce, and John Henry a cheery sendoff as they rented a vehicle to drive stateside to pick up the company's first piece of equipment. We had already secured an office that included warehouse space, and once the new equipment was delivered, one might say the prophetic promise over our lives had been birthed.

Over the next few years, the business would experience exponential growth, and many prophetic words would continue to confirm to us that our business was destined to create finances for "God's Kingdom purposes." John Henry had a creative and entrepreneurial mind, and he would develop and patent ideas into products and even work for Disney. We didn't have to go looking for ways to grow; growth seemed to find us as the business grew quickly. More business meant more machines, which meant more employees, which always meant more money. And more money meant more investors and more bank loans. It was said that our business was one of the fastest growing companies in that industry in Western Canada. It felt like the words being spoken over us were alive and full of power. We believed we were God's Kingdom people.

It's with your feet that you move ... but it's with your heart that you dance.

—The Dance Bible

16

JUST DANCE

Prophetic dance became the central focus of my life. It was the heart of my being that steadied and centred me, and everything else radiated outward from it. I believed it was part of God's purpose and plan for my life. I continued to raise my children, as they were still young; I even had them take part in a prophetic dance when I was asked to choreograph a dance for the Watchmen for the Nations tour across Canada. Watchmen for the Nations is an international Christian movement committed to fostering unity, intercession, and spiritual awakening across the globe. I no longer had spare time—I became focused. I felt I had a mission, and in some ways, my normal self and my goal-setting got to take centre stage. My exploration of the mystical realm united words and movement together, infused with Heaven's thick presence. I bathed myself in this realm. Soaking myself, songs played on repeat, over and over, hours at a time. Time was suspended as I entered a realm where choreography was created in my mind. Believing I was bringing Heaven to Earth, I sought *rhema*'s illumination as I pieced together people, props, colours, and songs. Fasting only intensified my ability to focus. I coveted my times in prayer searching for signs to confirm my choices. Once such decision was determining who was chosen by God to be on this initial prophetic dance team.

I believed God was overseeing everything. One of the most exciting events on the horizon was that our church had decided to host a women's conference. There was a buzz in the congregation among the women who had attended the conference in Edmonton, and it was decided that we would host one too. Not only was the prospect of hosting a conference exciting, but prophetic dance was to be part of this conference and Claire Hunter herself would be returning to Canada as our conference speaker. All of it felt like confirmation that I was being rewarded for my service to God, and I truly believed only good things were ahead.

For this conference, Katheryn, my closest friend, was put in charge, and she created a team that would oversee various roles. It was an exciting time in our church, as it was usually the men who led these kinds of events. But this time, it was the women, and most of the women in the church rallied together to prepare for the conference. In our Mennonite church, even though our congregation was small in number, we were large in heart, and it was common for everyone to lend a hand. But seeing as many of the wives were busy with at the church, it was beginning to cause conflicts at home for some.

Just prior to the conference, Pastor Rowan called a meeting for the men. Something was up. The outcome of the men's meeting was something of a surprise; I received an apology for not feeling supported through the process of getting ready for the conference. *Wow! This is new.* It was a nice slight change of pace.

The time came for our first women's conference; by Saturday evening, we had standing room only with approximately two hundred people in attendance. We had prepared both solo and duet performances, and we would end with a finale that included all five of us dancers. In number symbology, the number five represented God's grace.

It was time for me to step out and minister in dance, desiring deeply to step into my purpose, but every inch of my body ached as I prepared to do my first solo. Flushing the toilet for the tenth time, I found myself speaking to my reflection in the bathroom mirror. "Susan, this is just a test. Remember, things are going to be hard, maybe even feel a bit desperate, but remember that breakthrough is on the other side!" Steadying myself, I adjusted my satin sash, put on my dance mask, and with those words in mind, I walked into the sanctuary. I danced with every fibre of my being. I danced as though Heaven had a front row seat. This dance was also a drama to the song "Freedom Reigns in This Place." I was transported. As I danced, I felt that weighty presence that comes when everyone is breathing in sync. It was profound to me that after I ministered in dance, I felt physically better, as if I was weightless and a warm electric current filled my body.

In between sessions, I found myself standing to the side of the entrance door to our sanctuary, which also doubled as a gym. Claire stopped as she was making her way into the sanctuary to speak to me. "Hello, Susan, correct?" I nodded, "Yes." Claire looked me straight in the eyes as though she could see into my soul, "Susan, when you danced, I want you to know that I felt something in the atmosphere break open. Your ministry in that dance was powerfully felt." When Claire spoke those words, I swear my heart skipped a beat. I took it as a sign. *See, it's all about breakthrough,* I said to myself, *next time, just keep pressing through and I'll be rewarded.* I also believed that Claire's words confirmed that the breaker anointing was alive and active in my life.

The session was about to start. I took my seat next to Mum. Mum had made a special trip to help with our children while we were at the conference, and she came to the morning session to see me minister in dance. However, Mum was not so enticed by Claire or her words. Mum's comment on the session was that that Claire only read a few Scriptures then spent the rest of the time sharing her spiritual revelations—this can be a typical response from someone who has always leaned more towards the Word rather than personal spiritual experiences, yet Mum had experienced both the Word and had spiritual experiences so I was taken off guard.

Everyone at the conference could feel the building momentum as the church was saturated with a new energy and enthusiasm; it felt as though a fresh wind was blowing through our bodies. By Saturday night, many of the members of the leadership team from the church in Edmonton joined us. Our dance team was prepared—we were intensely focused. As we entered the sanctuary, it felt as though we ushered in wave after wave of anointing, it was as though Heaven was responding to our surrender and our passion. Our procession, with the use of flags, seemed thick, holy, yet triumphant. The shift in the atmosphere was not manufactured, we just made room for God to be in our midst.

"Susan, how did you choose those who got to dance in this conference? Why didn't you make an announcement to the whole congregation?" I was asked more than once. As best I could, my answer was, "I prayed and asked God who He wanted to be on this initial dance team, but don't worry, there's a lot more coming," believing that God had already shown me the who, what, when, and how.

When Sunday came, instead of having a dance prepared for the Sunday morning service, we free danced, and as the dancers danced, I took the microphone and said, "If you are in the church today and want to experience the power of dance, I invite you to come up, take a flag, and begin to move your body for God." My invitation was the spark that lit a fire in our church as a new movement was created—the women wanted liberation!

There were two things I distinctly remember thinking during the week after the conference.

First, I felt as though every fibre of my being was alive, I felt incredibly seen and validated by God and by those in authority. I felt significant in God's eyes as I embodied a felt sense of meaning and purpose. Weave all this together and they created intense and powerful feelings (or should I say, attachments). I felt aligned to what I was destined to do. I felt powerful and powerfully used by God for the first time. Something that had been missing all my life suddenly felt so real.

Second, I knew that I wanted to be just like Claire. No. I wanted to be Claire, and from that day forward, I went through another season of change, but this time, my style, my tone, and how I prophesied would change to mirror Claire, the prophetess I deeply admired.

Threads I hold,
All Velcro Kisses, Susan. See the power of indoctrination?
The power of connection? In every situation, one can look
at both the positive and the negative, but right now, you
only see and experience one side of the coin. The sweet side

of the coin is the side of life where one feels that they are chosen, seen, valued, and have a special purpose on Earth for God. This is where you get special assignments and gifts from God, and everything seemed to be confirmed by those who are leaders in the body of Christ. You are perceived as someone who can pray and prophesy over the lives of others, and you are able to minister to their spirits and souls.

Life seems so good that you can't imagine being anywhere else or doing anything different than what you're doing now. You can't imagine life being different. But it's love bombing at its finest and you are attaching so deeply that its going to be painful as you detach from these people. You can't imagine anything going wrong—you are on a high. In this place, you have yet to see that just as there were incredible highs there will also be incredible lows. Susan, I wish you had known this, because if you did, you might not be so eager to take on this upcoming responsibility. Out-side voices are amplified as you turned down the volume on your own voice. And in a time of upcoming loss and confusion, hurt follows.

On the other side of the coin, self-doubt and confusion will make thoughts blurry as your mind searches the Scriptures for God's rhema words for answers. Your mind will begin to ping pong between opposing views, also known as cog-nitive dissonance. Once you learn about cognitive disso-nance and understand what it does to your brain, you will have taken a step to begin to heal and empower yourself. In time, Susan, you will come to know, very clearly, that the answer always was "That was definitely not God!"

Pleasure and pain are the two sides. One side is visible at a time. But remember the other side is waiting for its turn.

—Daily Inspiration Quote

17

CRACKS

We were in business for a few years, and left unchecked, as the business grew, more and more cracks appeared—this time relationally. Even though we were cemented into our church community—there was something about cement I was about to learn—under the wrong circumstances, cement can crack due to something called drying shrinkage, which can be caused by internal stressors and, like cement with internal stressors, we were about to experience intense circumstances that would create cracks in our lives, our relationships, my ministry, and our business.

Even though we had been at Pineridge for many years, all the side-stepping issues were occurring more consistently and becoming much more dangerous. Our business had become a prime target for repeated break-ins because of the location. Company computers and equipment were stolen on multiple occasions. It seemed like prayer wasn't going to yield a solution, nor did the police seem to be able to find the culprits. Because of the continued break-ins, it was decided that moving our business to a larger building would be the solution, which meant more space, more staff could be hired, and more machines could be purchased. Our business focused on producing materials and meeting deadlines. With more growth came more pressures, and with more pressures, the cracks in our relationships fractured more than ever before.

The main fracture came the day my husband and I were called into Pastor Rowan's office to discuss an employee and his family. "John Henry and Susan, I've had another conversation with Ron and his wife. They've come to me because he said he's afraid to talk with you about some of the things you've done. You know they just purchased a new home, and he is counting on some extra promises that you've made to him," Pastor Rowan relayed. "What are you talking about, Rowan? Ron never came to us and we didn't ask them to go out and purchase a new house." The conversation continued. It was clear the situation was triangular, with Pastor Rowan taking the top point. Our employee, instead of going to my husband, would go to our pastor and share their grievances, then our pastor would call my husband and I into his office to discuss the disputes. This situation was an obvious red flag to any business owner, and all it did was make me furious at our employees. Keep in mind that at that time, I believed emotions could be used by the Enemy, so I tried to negate any negative feelings I had and instead prayed for God to intervene on our behalf. Finally, we decided to seek advice from someone other than our pastor.

In another meeting about our company, Pastor Rowan opened saying, "God has given me a insight into what is happening in your business. God's shown me a picture somewhat like a two-headed monster." "What are you talking about? Why? Because we asked Pastor Rafe what God was showing him?" we asked. No answer came and our meeting quickly ended. Differing opinions. Do we believe the two-headed monster insight, or do we believe what Rafe said which was that a religious spirit was attacking our company? In that moment, like a seed planted in my chest, the feeling began to grow and I began to realize we might be facing the beginning of the end.

Our business's fall from grace was slow and painful. We had been in business for five years and had multiple investment surges. Many people invested after hearing the prophetic words spoken over us. Many more invested after they saw the business growth that we experienced. And many close friends and family invested because of their relationship with each of us.

When I look back now, I see how so many of us were all so trusting, playing in a big game of prophetic roulette and the stakes were high, very high. And cost it did. Dearly. Relationships were destroyed, homes were possessed by the bank, and the church was torn. For me, the realization of God's dream for our life was about to be dismantled piece by piece. Our family would not have survived this season if we didn't have those closest to us love and support us.

The nail in the coffin came one evening at the church as a microphone stood in the front of the sanctuary and one by one, church members, investors, and employees would stand and share the *rhema* word that God had spoken to them.

"As I was praying today, God showed me that there is going to be seven years of famine and to prepare."

"This will be a tough season, but God will turn this into something good."

"Just as Joseph had to go through a season of surrender and had to endure testing, God too asks you to surrender as this test comes your way."

"Know this, that He will bring restoration on the other side," spoke another.

"God has shown me that He's going to walk you through the process of the cross."

"And just as Jesus bore the shame, your business will as well, but know this, that in due time, God will raise you back up and infuse you with new life," another member spoke into the microphone.

"God wants to do miracles!"

"Stand strong in this season!"

"God is going to act on your behalf and bring defeat to the Enemy who is trying to attack your business," one of our closest friends spoke into the microphone.

Each person, taking their turn, spoke in the microphone, declaring what God said to them about our business. From the words I heard, I believed, no I *knew* that God was done with us. It was as though the God who I spoke to in the car as a little girl was still not going to let me get a chance at life, no matter how hard I tried. In the church that night, there were clearly two differing views about what God had to say about the business. Each person believed they heard God. Each person aligned with a side. That was the day, I believe, the business died; something died, that's for sure.

In my mind, I could feel my two selves breaking down in their own ways; my normal self took notes on how it would seem that the years of investment disappeared overnight. That all the work I did to find belonging—the ladders I climbed, the visions I defined, and the goals I reached—was now being torn away. My normal self watched and listened as God and His Word were being weaponized and used against our business, highlighting that those people who I had come to identify as "family" were now beginning to pull away. Threads that were weaved in friendship, in community, and in the name of God detached themselves from me. This feeling of ostracization and isolation was painfully familiar. My spiritual self only saw deeply held fears. Fears that were connected to survival, fears that were connected to God. All these words packed a punch. My spiritual self was spinning, questioning every narrative, feeling the weight and guilt of the harm and disruption I had inflicted.

Threads I hold,
I'm grateful that you and your family had the support of such good friends. I'm grateful that you did the work and had the courage to keep trying in life and at life especially after all this. In the future, you will sit with Andy and Bruce and their families. You will once again have meals together and Andy will reassure you that they are okay, they are doing well and have recovered much, and they even own their own home again. Andy will say these words to you personally, "Susan, I need to say this to you because you carried so much for everyone." As Andy says those words, they will begin to unburden you. The final time that you will speak with Andy will be in 2024, as Andy will pass away in this sleep soon after. You followed your intuition as it guided you to reach out to Andy, it wasn't in a prophetic word that led you to do so; it was a intuitive sensing, an insistent nudge inside of you.

Gut feeling, intuition, the voice in your heart, listen to it more. Trust yourself.

—The Universe

18

TRYING TO CONNECT THE DOTS

I emailed one of the lasts prophets who came to our church—a prophetess who prophesied that God was going to use our business to bring finances into the Kingdom. My first question to her was, "What happened? You just spoke this word over us and look at what's happening now." The prophetess's reply was, "You grew too fast." *That's it?* I couldn't wrap my mind around her answer, "You couldn't have given us any warning? Told us about it then vs. now?" I questioned. Needless to say, our conversation fizzled out soon thereafter. Within a day or two, I received an email and in it, she shared how God had once stripped her of everything, saying that she had placed too much importance on earthly possessions. *Was that what I was doing wrong? Did I have too much pride? Did I like "things" too much?* We still lived on the same farm site that we moved to when we began the business, I drove a new-to-me vehicle, and I bought my children's clothes at children's consignment stores. Yet, because I believed this person spoke on God's behalf, I put more emphasis on what she said rather than any thought of my own.

If you were to ask a hundred people what happened to our business, I believe you would likely get many different answers. Answers would vary depending on if that person was in our church, a close family member, a friend, or an employee. What I've shared is simply my opinion.

I remained at Pineridge after the close of our business and even tried to continue my sense of belonging with many of the same people who had judged me. Remember, my attachment to this community was wholehearted, and I was all in. I didn't think of it as a disorganized or anxious attachment style. I thought that showing my loyalty to this community, to these relationships, would bring healing, but it didn't—because it can't. In these environments, it can only become undue loyalty.

There was a twelve-month period around 2003 that was particularly difficult as we watched our business be pulled apart piece by piece, and I too would find myself in front of lawyers preparing for bankruptcy. I may not have had a home, but I used everything else I had, and with my credit cards maxed out, I couldn't recover financially. With loss all around us, John Henry and I separated to process, or ignore, our own grief. Instead of processing this loss together, we created a cycle of deflection and blame that would continue to define our relationship until its eventual end years later. Yet, for now, we remained together out of a deep desire to keep our family intact and to finally materialize breakthrough in our lives. We pushed and pressed our way through the year and a half until our breakthrough came! It was an opportunity for John Henry—this time, in the United States—and we took it.

Threads I hold,
Attachment styles should be course 101 in the school of life skills. Understanding and seeing how attachment affects every relationship is vital information for everyone. Because of your childhood, you developed a blend of

attachment styles, and in this context, you connect with both disorganized and anxious attachment styles, which makes you an easy target for undue loyalty.

Some call it blind obedience, but undue loyalty is also when you are required to overlook the wrongdoings of those in the group and can lead to self-abandonment to one's truth or integrity. In a spiritual setting, as there was a spiritual aspect to the business, it can manifest when you are more loyal to a person, community, even God's leading than you are to yourself. Your loyalty is no longer rooted in truth, but in fear: fear of loss, fear of rejection, or even fear of being ripped out from under your covering. Blind obedience, ignoring wrongdoings, neglecting self-care, family disfunction, business issues—you had many of the symptoms. But in the future, you will come to learn and embody healthy loyalty, which is rooted in love, truth, and freedom. It involves support and mutual respect. It includes the ability to think critically, examine situations, ask questions, and create boundaries. It is normal to prioritize your own well-being. Healthy loyalty comes out of discerning what is right and true for you, not fear. This is one of your biggest lessons.

Every new beginning comes from some other beginning's end.

—Seneca

19

FAILING FORWARD

The year 2003 was a season I like to call failing forward. Securing our breakthrough would require money, money we didn't have, so we borrowed enough funds from my sister saying we would repay her as soon as we could. A friend sent us a book called *Failing Forward* by John C. Maxwell when our business finally closed. Reading that book changed our perspective. Not completely, but enough to get a new point of view. With the support of my sister and our closest friends, we were able to pick up the pieces and borrow enough courage to dare to believe again.

John Henry travelled to the US, and I would remain behind and continue each Sunday to attend Pineridge. In the same church where we used to sit in the front row as a family, I now took my seat in the back row. No one moved me; I moved myself. Each Sunday, I found myself watching the church service, and with each new service, I felt more and more like an outsider.

That same year, John Henry began to consult in the US and we would find ourselves relocating back to the city, this time to the lake community of Lake Chaparral. It seemed more than a coincidence—it was a sign of another new beginning.

We also made the decision to put our children into a private Christian school since I had been homeschooling up until that point. Making these changes allowed me to have more time in my day as I attempted to process everything that happened. I didn't think to see a professional to help process all this at the time. I did what I knew; I sought God.

Your perspective will either become your prison or your passport.

—Steven Furlick

20

OH SHIT

Putting my children in Christian school allowed me to meet other moms from different church communities, and one of these moms was Bess. Bess had recently moved from Ontario to Alberta, and we struck up a friendship as soon as we met. Bess came out of the Vineyard background; she talked about God as a Father, about the love of God, and how much we were loved. Bess reminded me of Judy. Bess and I would languish in our conversations around God, His grace and what that all meant to us. It felt as though there was a gravitational shift in the ground underneath our feet as I leaned into every word Bess shared.

Then, Sunday would arrive, and the ground would shift again as I returned to my old church still attempting to find acceptance. One Sunday, as I sang in worship, I could feel a fresh wind coming in my direction, it seemed to carry thoughts of who I used to be and who I was becoming. I found myself connecting to bravery, self trust, and the power of new beginnings. I felt God's grace. I could feel the difference in the air and that difference was palpable—my body felt completely different. Our closest friends had already left the church and I was sensing—no, more than sensing—I was beginning to believe that there was another life outside of those four walls and that community. I was beginning to wonder if I would give myself the permission I needed to leave that church, but before I could, I believed I needed my pastor's blessing to have the confidence to leave and start fresh.

The day arrived for me to meet with my pastor. John Henry had asked me if I wanted him to be there when I met with Pastor Rowan, but felt that I had this one, as our pastor had already announced from the pulpit that John Henry was no longer in eldership. I trusted my relationship with Pastor Rowan—he had worn many hats throughout my time at Pineridge Christian Fellowship: from counsellor to spiritual father to being the prophetic voice in our church. Having his blessing as I left was very important to me, especially to my spiritual self, as even though I would have never admitted it at the time, Pastor Rowan was one of the main ways God spoke to me.

The time of our meeting arrived. I stood at Pastor Rowan's office door prepared. "Hi Pastor Rowan, thank you for seeing me. I asked to meet with you because I wanted to share what I believe God has placed on my heart. I know that there's been a lot of change in the church lately, but I want you to know that I was sensing this for sometime before Mike and Katheryn left. I sense that God wants me to come out from my father's house and to go on my own and begin to hear Him more on my own."

Pastor Rowan looked my squarely in the eyes and said, "Well, God hasn't said that to me. And I don't want you to go out before you're ready for it. Yes, it was time for Mike and Katheryn to leave. They've done a lot of work, but you—you need to stay. You're not ready and it's my job to protect you."

I took in every word he spoke. I took a deep breath, "I truly feel that God is calling me out. I can always go, and, if

I find that I can't make it, then maybe I could come back?" It was both a comment and a question.

Pastor Rowan leaned in and said, "Look, I was just reading about Jezebel this morning … and no woman is going to come in here and tell me what God is saying."

Stunned by the words I just heard, I tried to find something to say, "But, I could try, and if I've made a mistake, then I could come back if I needed to," I almost pleaded.

Without hesitation, Pastor Rowan seized the moment and said, "If you leave, your ministry is done!"

I felt like a child again, frozen in time. *Did I just hear correctly? Did I actually hear God? Was it my time to leave my father's house and come under the Lord's direction? Was this even biblical?* For a moment, I thought of pleading my case, but the next words I heard were "Go! You can go, but you cannot come back whenever you want. If you go, you're gone." These were the final words I remember.

My spiritual self was reeling, it all felt so familiar—emotionally, I was right back at that table as Simon forced me to recite the Sinner's prayer. My spiritual self never wanted to be in this place again, as it had just spent the last decade looking for signs and reassurances that God was not angry with me. But how could God not be angry with me if He let me have that meeting with Pastor Rowan? Black-and-white thinking sucker punched me in the face again. Finally, I gathered myself enough to walk out the front door, and as I opened the door, I let it swing wide open saying out loud, "God, either I'm hearing you, or I just signed my own death warrant."

And then it registered, "Oh shit!"

Threads I hold,
Whew! Black-and-white thinking, systems of control, au-
thoritarian groups, us vs. them labels, punitive actions if
one goes against the thoughts of the leader ... all part of
coercive control. You couldn't see it then, but I see it clearly
now. Then, you were reeling in what most people who come
out of these structures struggle with: the shock, the trauma,
the disenfranchised grief. That is, until they find help and
begin to tell their stories to find the words they need to take
back their narratives. This will come for you, but not yet,
you still think this only happened to you. Symptoms will
continue to show up in your life, you will continue to go to
churches that lean heavily into the prophetic, into spiritual
warfare, and into intercession. In these churches, people
who are considered prophets will see your trauma, speak
of the trauma you just experienced, yet the only solution
they will offer is going to prayer and to God. Spiritual
bypassing and magical thinking are offered as prescriptive
measures when what you need, and what does help you in
the future, is trauma-informed therapy that identifies and
helps you process the trauma cognitively, emotionally, and
physically.

EMDR, also known as eye movement desensitization
and reprocessing, will help you digest these traumas as your
brain becomes more and more integrated. Neuroscience will
help you understand how your brain was impacted. Somat-
ic work will help process these experiences as your nervous
system begins to regulate. Learning about attachment styles
will be instrumental in helping you begin to unwind all

those lived experiences and will show you how the threads were weaved and with which hook. You will begin the process of detaching and begin to design from the inside out the life you want. Until then, you will continue to experience triggers and re-activations, especially when you are in environments, groups, and relationships where you have sensitivities to rejection, exclusion, and the demands of loyalty and dependency.

At this point, you're still believing that these people or groups are protecting you from harm, that they are somehow keeping your soul safe, and that "they" know about your future successes. I ask you to look at what was said that made you give your trust away: What did they say or do to get you to look to them and lean on them for answers? Was it fear, or was it their charisma? Was it the energy in the room? Trusting "them" over yourself continues to foster dependency and people pleasing rather than following your own intuition and inner guidance. Some therapists call this an external locus of control rather than an internal locus of control. This dependent state that has been encouraged will keep you looking for answers outside of yourself and even causes you to gaslight yourself as you try to make decisions on your own in the future. It happens so subtly that you don't even realise that it is happening until one day you wake up to what it has cost you and your family for following all those voices that are not yours. Your healing lies in learning that, yes, it may be helpful to have people in your life who are safe, who will play a role that helps you come to your own answers rather than have the answer. As you learn and practise this foundational skill, no longer will you try to move forward in life handicapped by dependency, or by the fear of loss, or the anxiety that comes with a differing perspective. You will gain this skill by making the time and space. Then, you will create the right kinds of support in your life, allowing you to work through your childhood emotional injuries, your adult traumas, and the religious and spiritual abuse you've experienced. By doing this work, you will come to clearly see what patterns and templates they have created in your life. This will be in the future. Here, right now, I want to say how sorry I am that you just had to experience this intense emotional and spiritual injury.

Spiritual abuse is emotional abuse cloaked in religious language.

—Emily Hendrick

21

STEPPING STONES

Reaching for my phone, I quickly dialed Bess. "Susan, are you okay?" Bess could tell as soon as I spoke that something was wrong. "Bess, the meeting with Pastor Rowan didn't go well. I can't even think right now, he said—" Bess interrupted, "Susan, come over, don't go home. Come, we can talk this through." "Okay, okay, I'll come."

The moment Bess saw my face, she was on a mission; Bess was determined to help me ground my spiralling thoughts and anchor myself back into the love of God. I couldn't process all the different fractures that just took place, nor did I have the words to describe what just happened. Emotions surged within, coming fast and furious; I was deaf to any logic. I was violated mentally, psychologically, and spiritually. My world had just shattered because in essence, I was just told that I could not, as a woman, trust that I was hearing God or feel the leading of the Holy Spirit. *Do I have options? Do I cave in, abandon myself, and let Pastor Rowan's words violate my sense of self?*

Unfortunately, I wasn't who I am today. So, I watched as Pastor Rowan pulled the threads, and as he did, he wove more confusion into my story—a story that began as a young girl in her mum's car. Even after a lifetime of going back and forth between my normal self and my spiritual self, being fully devoted, all in, on fire, I still didn't have access to God in a way that fostered comfort, grace, or self trust. Here I was in my thirties, and yet I felt like that little six-year-old girl. Was Pastor Rowan any different than Simon? And why is it that then and now, it's men who gatekeep women's access to God?

I spent days meaning-making and searching God's Word for a *rhema* word that might guide me. I devoured every book I could find desperately seeking for answers. I would continue to seek out prophets for a word from the Lord about what just happened and what to do next. My trust in my ability to hear God was shattered; something broke inside me in that meeting, leaving me unsure if I *ever* really heard God. Seeking out environments and meetings where there were well-known established prophets became my lifeline. I believed that my solution was to seek some reassurance from the source that just hurt me because the rejection that I had just experienced didn't register. The rejection went deep, and I was making decisions that were not all that different from those in abusive romantic relationships. I needed validation or at least some reassurance that my source of truth and sense of self wasn't completely gone.

My seeking paid off, as in January 2004, I would be called out and receive a prophetic word from a young man who was already well-known and established in prophetic circles, both in Canada and internationally. This was his word to me. He did not know me; we had never met before. He was preaching a message on boldness.

> *There's a boldness. Release a boldness to become a fearless lover for it's only fear that keeps us from the world. What if they don't like me? What if they reject me? The anointing can come on what your personality is and make your supernaturally bold.*

Then, he called me out of a crowd of about 500 people and spoke this word over me.

This woman right here in the black—you, stand up. There's a boldness that's going to come upon your life to take the gift of prophecy of being able to see, hear visions and dreams that the Holy Spirit is about to release on you and take that right out to people on the street right into Tim Hortons/Starbucks. I don't know where you work or if you work with kids or been in any kind of teaching type setting or anything like that but there's an anointing upon your life for teaching and preaching and it's going to be amongst young people and there's some leadership mantle on you right now and I see groups of young people even if it's only eight and I see you walking up to them and saying you know what, I want to pray for you and you're going to break out into this spiritual reading thing and break out into this prophecy thing that you're going to have in your heart—"let's get a group of women together," "let's go into the street on Saturday," and "let's get to the Starbucks," and "let's give kids words," and there's just going to be an anointing that's going to come upon your life for that. I want you to say, "Yes, Holy Spirit." That's what I want. "I want something of your presence to come upon my life and begin to release the realm of dreams." You might even dream about it the night before you go. And you'll go out into the marketplace and say, "Listen, I saw that kid in my dream last night." Walk up to them and say, "I have the word of the Lord," so you have the whole prophetic gift on your life. That mantle's going to come on your life of prophecy, and you're just going to get visited with this spirit of prophecy. I don't know how much you've operated in it before but here, just a shaking and a wind that's coming of prophecy on your life and it's because you're going to prophesy to the bones that are dead like Ezekiel 47. You're going to command them to live, they'll rattle, come together, and flesh, and it's going to be among young people. I see groups of young people that's why I ask you if you're in any kind of school or university type setting because I keep seeing these campuses and groups of young people but even out in the marketplace, the malls, and doughnut shop—the places where God is going to move you, even at ten o'clock at night—boldness that's going to come on you because there's a prophecy that hasn't been stirred in your life and it's time to stir. You know what—there's been a shutting down, there's been a shutting down, there's been things that would come up but I tell you what it is: a season of releasing, releasing, releasing, releasing, releasing, and recommissioning, recommissioning, reconnecting, and stirring, and stirring, and stirring the gift of God and I release you right now in Jesus's mighty name. God is taking the cap off of the quenching and He's gonna say it's okay to be free, it's okay to have a voice again, I release you to speak again in Jesus's mighty name.

His words carried a charge that lit up every fibre in me, my body shaking uncontrollably, electrified from the inside out. It was as though I had frostbite. Frozen by fear to thoughts that God had abandoned me, that He had left me out in the cold, but now receiving this prophetic word was the fire that provided the heat that allowed me to feel again. The room felt like it tilted, or maybe it was just me. I needed assistance to stand, it took hours to regain my composure. Everyone around me was wishing they had been given the word I had just received.

The woman a few seats away said to her friend, "I feel like that word could have been for me too." So, when there was an altar call at the end of this meeting to "catch the boldness" God wanted to release, still glued to where I was standing, I watched as this same woman pushed her way to the front of the stage. When I did gain my composure to walk, it felt as though courage returned to my bones and I began to walk upright again, feeling that God was once again on my side. The weight of the trauma that I had experienced was beginning to loosen its grip on me.

11:11—speaks. Three months from now, you will be in a completely different place, mentally, spiritually, financially.

—The Secret

22

YOU HAVE BEEN FAITHFUL

Not long after I left Pineridge Church, Pastor Rowan stepped down from his role as head pastor and unfortunately passed way suddenly. The story I was told was that Pastor Rowan was invited to speak in another church in our city and once he finished preaching, he took his seat, leaned over onto his wife, and passed. But, before he passed away, Pastor Rowan phoned me and on that phone call, he apologized for how things turned out between us and wished my family well. "I will always look to you as my spiritual father, Pastor Rowan, and I too am sorry for the way things turned out between us." Those were my last words.

As life would have it, while my family and I were attending another church in the city, our new church partnered with Pineridge to host a conference with a well-known prophetic minister. And so, there I was, about to step back into my old church. I was committed to showing that I wanted to make things right, especially considering they had a new pastor.

Prophetic dance once again became a medium for purpose and meaning. One of my previous dance team members and friend agreed to choreograph a dance with me specifically for her church and this conference. I brought the music and together, we choreographed a dance that spoke of the power of unity that displaces judgement and competition. As we ministered, the sanctuary was wrapped in a holy hush.

As we danced, a silence like a whispered prayer began to fill the air carrying the tangible presence of the Spirit. No one moved once the song ended; it felt as though Heaven itself had entered the sanctuary. Finally, Prophet Gerald rose from his seat. Taking the microphone, he said quietly, "It feels as though God Himself has entered the room," wiping tears from his face. Looking around, it wasn't only Prophet Gerald; it looked like a sea of tears. As healing was taking place, the walls that were built around our hearts and spirits began to crumble. I could feel those feeling I used to know, the ones I thought I had lost, that warmth, assurance, and certainty that comes with being used by God in a powerful way, where time is suspended and all there is this present moment where your purpose feels crystal clear as God works through you. I knew God had something *big* planned.

On the final morning of the conference, as customary with this prophet and his ministry, he would ask the pastors if they knew someone who "needs a word from the Lord" and have them bring those people to the front of the church. We were "one of those people"; our pastors came to us and brought us to the front of the church and Prophet Gerald began to speak a prophetic word over us. Prophet Gerald often said that when he prophesied, it was as though a screen would appear in front of him, and he simply spoke about what he saw. As the prophetic word was released over our lives that day, it was as though the word *breakthrough* had wrapped itself around us. Prophet Gerald spoke about things we had never shared publicly. Having this word prophesied over us, John Henry and I could once again set our sights on God and God's Kingdom. Feeling once again that we were given purpose and mission in life, this word would become "our word" for the next season of our life and remembered as the 2004 prophetic word.

When I was speaking about kings—there's a commission on your heart. And your spirit wondered if it dared believe again. Dare, believe again! Dare, believe again. For the call both within the Kingdom and to minister—minister broadly. It's within you and yet it was killed three times. It was destroyed three times and you wondered—could it live again? YES—Bones, live! Bones, live! Bones, live! Come alive and rule! Come alive and rule! Such wealth, such wealth, will flow through your lives because I can count you worthy now. And you died within, and you let it go willingly, but then you wondered—did you fail? You did not fail. There was one relationship where it was violated. That person did not know how to deal with things. And there was even an unfairness and injustice inside of them and people suffer because of injustices. And yet, you had to push through but there was a spiritual wall that you conquered—well, the curse stops here. You are on the other side of it so you can be a king and a queen to make things happen. And yet, you had to abandon things, and you ripped out. Some did not understand you—well, this year, I give you the favour of your extended family and they will begin to respect your walk with me and things are turning around. A risk, a risk, and investment. You follow through because you have wisdom now when to do it and you have my confidence. Watch and see. Watch and see the incredible door through the states and finances and wealth flow. Watch and see up here. But doors will open in the south terrifically for you. And woman of God, bring into the Earth the grace that only you can bring. Bring into the Earth only the grace you can bring. And when you are with those of influence, you will shepherd them and the two of you will influence them who have political influence, financial influence, and business world, that's where I'm taking you now this year. And I can trust you with it. I can trust you with it. And woman, you didn't give up. You didn't give up. And you are right. There's a prophetic edge to your life—bring that into the Earth and don't be afraid of it. Jab him when he needs it—hold him on course this time. It's gonna work this time. It will work this time! It will work this time! Two years of labour, two years of planning, plowing the ground. Fruitfulness, fruitfulness, fruitfulness. Fruitfulness beyond your imagination will be granted to you. Yes, there's labour—but I know what to do now. And you have been faithful in Jesus's name.

I believed then that only God could orchestrate this moment on that day as we were embraced by those who had rejected us. We spent the afternoon gathered around a table, sharing a meal, our lives, and the time we lost. As our family left the restaurant that day, it was if new life had been poured into us and was beginning to flow.

People, even more than things, have to be restored, renewed, revived, reclaimed, and redeemed; never throw out anyone.

—Audrey Hepburn

23

REBIRTH

John Henry continued to consult in the US, and I began to embrace my life in a new way. It was a season of rebirth. I now had living proof that what Pastor Rowan said to me that day in our meeting in his office wasn't true, or maybe I had been granted a divine reprieve. In the new church, my pastors urged me not to give up; they championed my continuation of prophetic dance, providing connections and opportunities within both the city and the nation, such as the Watchmen for the Nations when they were courting a spiritual romance between Quebec and the rest of Canada. I was invited to choreograph a dance. I gathered a friend from the dance ministry and her husband and my two young children and together we danced in Stephen Avenue Mall, joining together with some of the dancers from Quebec. We may not have shared a language, but we had the language of Heaven. In our dance, we joined yards of red, white, and blue fabric that was attached to a wooden cross together and as we weaved our way back and forth, we believed that something was happening in the Heavens. The weaving of the fabric was displayed in churches and cities they went on to—threads of unity and Heaven's mandate for our country.

In this season of rebirth, I opened myself up to new and various types of prophetic teachers. Graham Cooke would speak about intimacy with God as though it was a two-way friendship; he defined prophecy as a lifestyle of hearing and partnering with God rather than just future-telling. Paul Keith Davis and Bobby Conner were prominent prophetic voices and were known for their emphasis on revival, prophetic ministry, and spiritual awakening. Kathy Walters was known for her emphasis on living in the supernatural realm as an integral part of the Christian experience, empowering believers to embrace the fullness of their spiritual inheritance in Christ, moving beyond religious traditions into a vibrant, experiential relationship with God. Within the NAR, there were well-known prophetic ministers such as Shawn Boltz, Patricia King, and Todd Bentley. These are just a few of the people that I began to follow and learn from.

No longer feeling limited to only one stream of Christianity, I gave myself permission to swim in the wide ocean of God, where His Spirit moved freely. I opened myself up to different kinds of worship; rather than the emphasis being on God, traditional hymns, or songs about spiritual warfare and declaring God's Word, I began to listen to songs with themes of intimacy with God, God's love, and healing. Worship leaders like Joanna McFadder and Misty Edwards, and Christian churches that produced music like Hillsong and Bethel Music made their way into my music playlists. More importantly, I began to connect outside of the church, finding employment that would enable me to work around my children's school schedule. I embraced my life, my children, my work, and created new friendships and community. I was embracing everyday life and activities that a woman my age and stage in life should have been focusing on. I was actually embracing my normal self again, or maybe it was a rebirthing of my normal self many years later.

John Henry would continue to split his time between Canada and the United States and his contract work would eventually take him to Indiana where he would open dialogue around our moving. John Henry had always felt that it would be better for our family in the US and we both knew we had a prophetic word about moving stateside. I was torn, seeing the wear in our marriage since our business closed, creating this new life for myself and my children, but the word prevailed, and we would soon have our answer. I was now attending another church, but it was still under the covering of Christian International (CI). I had now built more space and places to connect in my life, so attending church wasn't a must each Sunday. But, when it came to conferences with well-known prophets, I couldn't resist.

On a Sunday morning in 2006, we went to church as a couple and received a prophetic word. This word wasn't as impactful as the previous one, but this word confirmed the direction and the abuse that I had experienced.

For the Lord would say to you, son and daughter, know that I'm doing new things within you. Son, I would say to you there was even a dream that was once within your heart. I'm resurrecting it even afresh and new. And it would have seemed that those dreams were dashed and gone into the ground for a season but I'm even breathing new life on it. And there's even change that I'm bringing even around about for you. And the Lord would say that it even felt like you were in a rut, and you've been faithful even in the little things even as it would seem to be what you would have called even some menial tasks. But you've been walking in my process over a period of time. And the Lord would say unto you daughter, you've been one who has had great strength and great stability, even been that strong prayer warrior ... And the Enemy would have had a plan to even destroy you and to take you out because of discouragement. But the Lord would say I even infused you with new hope and even with supernatural strength of My Spirit, the Lord would say unto you son and daughter, I'm about ready to catapult you even into this next season of your life that I have for you ... I'm about ready to bring you to a new season of transition and new season of release even in some areas of ministry, but even in some areas of function even in business ... you to be strong ministers in the marketplace but yet you shall be those ones who shall be that strength of ministry, even be those strong ministers even within the church because there is an anointing upon you to lay foundations in peoples' lives and there's an anointing upon you to even break open the pathway ... The Lord would say, daughter know that there is even truth I've revelated to you and I'm opening up your eyes of your understanding of spiritual matters and even in intercession and in that place of prayer there's even a strong discerning of spirits that I've placed within you and there's a strong prophetic anointing a strong prophetic call and it would have seemed for a season of time that you would have even been set on a shelf, you would have been sat by because there would have been those who would have even discarded you and laid you aside even in some disappointment and some trauma even of past days ... And the Lord would say know son and daughter you're about ready even to walk into that new place and even the release of the promise that I had originally gave you and know that I am restoring to you even that which the Enemy robbed. The Enemy came in to rob, kill, and destroy for a season, but the

Lord would say know that I am even infusing with new life to you in the realm of the Spirit and in the natural and I am even restoring even your fortune. Surely know that even as I have turned your captivity this is a season that I am restoring your fortunes back to you. That was the Enemy that robbed and even the hand of man to even rob from you, this is a season that I am causing restoration to come to all things.

And with this word my husband and I believed that this was God's Spirit taking us south, and in so doing, God would restore everything that the Enemy had stolen from us.

Threads I hold,

Did you ever wonder why these prophets could "see" trauma yet never heal the trauma? Why was it that spiritual bypassing played such a big role in healing one's self? Do spiritual words heal trauma? Relational trauma needs to be healed in relationship. Person-to-person therapy, support groups in community, and trauma-informed coaching are just a few things required. Have you noticed how so many spiritual communities mention trauma in relation to the Enemy, to destruction, or to something trying to take one out? Spiritual bypassing is used, and trauma becomes a tool of the Enemy rather than something that is done by other people to other people. Where is the accountability? The responsibility? Where is the feeling of safety in believing that one needs to continuously lean in, press in, and push through while one is still bleeding from all these emotional wounds? All in the name of breakthrough? You, Susan, will seek relief from the circumstances you found yourself in rather than seeking healing from the wounding you had experienced. One prophet jokingly—yet not so jokingly—said that his real name is Colander because of all the stab wounds he's had from the body of Christ saying, "Wounding is all just part of training for reigning in God's Kingdom." Is it?

I can't change the direction of the wind, but I can adjust my sails.

—Dolly Parton

24

VALPARAISO

With a renewed passion for God, I kept up my prophetic habit of looking for patterns—especially in numbers. On January 1, 2007, we crossed the border: a new year, a new beginning. I remember how I interpreted the date back then. January was the first month of the year, the first day of the month, and the number one represented God. As for the year 2007, the number two stood for multiplication, while seven symbolized perfection, completion, or fullness. Crossing the boarder on January 1, 2007 symbolized to me that God is saying we have completed (brought to fullness) one season and that God is creating a new beginning for our family. The moving truck hauling all our belongings had *Kings Transportation* written in big letters on the side—you can't make that up. Back then, I took it as absolute proof that God was guiding every mile as we crossed the border.

We arrived in Valparaiso and settled into a new home that was surrounded by water on two sides. In the yard, at the water's end, were two willow trees, which is my favourite type of tree. Willow trees remind me of life's beauty as they dance gracefully through the breeze. Sitting on the deck in the oversized wicker chairs listening to the songbirds, a soft playlist by nature itself, I felt as though I entered a storybook, especially when the fireflies came out. It truly was magical. By Christmas of that year, we were pinching ourselves at the thought that life could be this good. We purposefully chose Valparaiso, Indiana as the town we wanted to live in, and from the moment I walked into the church, I felt like I was home. The music, though Vineyard-based, carried a prophetic undertone. Then, without our prior knowledge to choosing our new home church, the church announced that they were leaving the Vineyard and forming an affiliation and relationship with Bethel Redding and their Global Legacy Network. Can I hear a hallelujah! I had heard about Bethel Redding and part of me had secretly wished that I could go there one day, but here I was, standing in a new country, in a new church, and Redding was going to be coming to me!

If you're not familiar, Bethel Redding is a non-denominational megachurch that originally was under the Assemblies of God before they became non-denominational. In 1995, Bill Johnson visited the revival meetings of the Toronto Blessing where he made the promise to God that he would make the outpouring of the Holy Spirit the sole purpose of his existence. Redding focuses on miracles, healing, prophecy, and encounters with God's presence. Bethel Redding is known for Bethel Music, whose songs are sung in many churches on Sunday mornings across North America, and for their Bethel School of Supernatural Ministry (BSSM) under the direction of Kris Vallotton. The school trains its student in the supernatural and miracles, such as faith healing, in order that they may become revivalists.

In some ways, it felt as though this was a full-circle moment in my life. Being connected to Bethel Redding opened my eyes to an entirely new perspective—that the Kingdom of Heaven can be experienced right here, right now, through people just like me. This heavy emphasis on experiencing God, feeling His presence, and partnering with the Holy Spirit on a daily basis made the supernatural seem natural again.

I had thought I was open to all that God had to offer, but I found myself needing to shift my mindset as I took in this new theology. My mind needed to reframe spiritual warfare, prophecy, and intercession, as Bethel taught it in a completely different way than what I previously believed. Being connected to Redding changed my life in ways I never expected. I didn't plan on entering another spiritual transformation, but being connected to this church, connected to Redding's teachings, awoke something in me, something I didn't know I was missing until I experienced it. I started to see myself, and God, differently than I had in Canada. I didn't have to manufacture how I connected to the supernatural—I opened myself to it. Connecting to God under this new teaching felt raw and honest in a profound way.

It was a turning point for me; it was almost as though God was beginning to write a new story rather than a new chapter in my life. I was no longer engaging in spiritual warfare as much; instead, I looked at my identity, who I was in God, and began to ask myself what was God's dream for my life. My life became about practising the presence of God, living a supernatural lifestyle, and establishing a mindset that was about Heaven invading Earth in ways that brought healing, peace, and solutions rather than constantly battling the spiritual forces of darkness to advance the Kingdom. I was royalty rather than a warrior. Worship became about hosting God's presence rather than war chants and strategic intercession. I became part of the Sozo ministry that came out of Bethel Church (Redding, California), which is an inner healing and deliverance ministry designed to help people experience personal freedom and a closer connection with God—with the Godhead: Father God, Jesus, and the Holy Spirit. In the Sozo ministry, a person is able to identify and heal wounds, lies, or blockages that might be interfering with a person's intimacy with God or other relationships. Participants are guided to uncover areas of past pain, trauma, or unforgiveness through prayer and dialogue. With the Sozo ministry came encounters to facilitate healing and deliverance rather than the hardcore laying-on-of-hands-type deliverance I was used to. It wasn't about prayers of repentance and teaching that my heart was desperately wicked, it was about opening my heart and letting healing in. For me, I felt many visceral shifts in perspectives, and I had many physical manifestations of God's presence without anyone touching me. Now, it's easy to see the draw of this movement and the hooks. As they say at Bethel, "History is HIS story."

Being connected to Redding felt as though I was stepping into a dream—the kind you don't want to wake up from because everything seemed more alive and more real than the world I knew. A dream that whispers to your heart, "This is what you were created for." As I allowed all this to soak in, wounds began to heal and the layers of shame began to peel away; for the first time in a long time, my life felt solid and sure.

Then came the financial crash of 2008. That, definitely, was not in our word about moving stateside!

We survived 2008 with a near miss of having to return to Canada. Being able to stay in the United States was important to us not only as a family but also prophetically. None of our words talked about returning to Canada—we had literally uprooted everything to follow God's word over our lives.

In 2008, John Henry was able to find a contract in Portland, Maine. That summer, the kids and I made a roundtrip investigating Kennebunkport and all the treasures that it brought. I found myself needing to remind myself to be present because I had been ruminating and going over and over the step-by-step process of how we came to the US and questioning if I had heard God correctly. *Why didn't any prophet warn us about the crash to come? Are we going to make it through this?* I had more questions than answers. I hadn't realized it was bringing up all those buried emotions around our previous business and its demise. My mind was caught on an old loop, one that would catch me up and take me away before I could ground my thoughts—it was a well-worn path, familiar but destructive.

I began leaning heavily into the new teachings I was learning, not just with my mind but also with my heart, searching for answers or solutions to the circumstances we had found ourselves in. By our second year in the US, I found myself bottoming out physically. Nothing I did seemed to lift the fatigue that I was feeling in my body. Every task felt heavier than it should've been, yet I kept going: taking the kids to school, returning home, crawling straight into bed, then dragging myself out again just in time to pick them up. I used what energy I had left to prepare dinner as I tried to give them the best of me. Over the span of one year, my body slowly degraded as it kept the score: first, my thyroid; then, my adrenals; and finally, a heart condition. One after the other, my body was sending signals I couldn't ignore anymore. This only added to my confusion because at the same time my body was breaking down, I was connecting to something that I loved—the supernatural lifestyle.

When your body says NO it doesn't matter how big your heart is.

—Gabor Maté

25

HEAVY HITTERS
AND DREAMS COME TRUE

Heavy hitters came to our church: Kris Vallotton, Danny and Sheri Silk, Brian and Jenn Johnson, Chris Gore, Joaquin Evans, and Kevin Dedmon, who shared that he received the mantle of Lonnie Frisbee, the signs-and-wonders evangelist of the Jesus Movement. Our church started a BSSM school, and we hosted many other speakers who would come to impart their knowledge. It was a huge all-you-can-eat buffet, except it was spiritual food and I was famished. I went to training sessions, joined teams, and took part in every available opportunity to immerse and embody these new teachings. I even started the BSSM school by video when the opportunity came. I was part of the "Friday Night Watches" that were part of the global prayer network, The Watch of the Lord under Mahesh and Bonnie Chavda, I was part of the prophetic team, the Sozo team, the conference team, and I continued to teach with flags in the arts. We made regular trips to Chicago to the Hub. My last trip to Chicago was to be in meetings with Kim Clement and Lance Wallnau, who were speaking on the Seven Mountain Mandate.

In a flash, 2008 turned into 2009 and we continued to seek God and what was prophesied over our lives. I kept landing on the words *risk* and *investment* from the 2004 prophetic word and the "two years of plowing, two years of planning."

In 2009, a close mentor and successful businessman in our church agreed to open an LLC and this allowed me to become certified in the Life Languages communication profile that John Henry had been using since the early 2000s. At the same time, we were given the opportunity to secure the rights to pioneer a Canadian program called the Heroes program, designed to build confidence and character through teaching resiliency skills to children and teens.

These new opportunities gave me the ability to do some things that I had always dreamed of doing in the business realm. As I sought God, I felt that this was the "risk" and "investment" that had been prophesied. I travelled to Dallas for my certification in Life Languages, and while there, I stayed in a hotel. It never really dawned on me that I was doing something unusual—leaving the bathroom light on, wedging a chair under the door—before I could even think about sleeping. I didn't pull back the sheets; I just laid on top of the bed and wrapped myself tightly in the hotel's spare blankets.

Strange, isn't it? Unprocessed trauma has a way of slipping through the cracks of time, resurfacing not in loud dramatic moments, but in those quiet automatic choices we make when our surroundings feel familiar. Here I was, years later, in a different city, believing I was living a different life, yet my body still remembered what my mind tried to forget.

Our new business took form and grew. We had the opportunity to meet with individuals, couples, small businesses, and leadership teams. I coached young women and loved seeing how they connected to both the profile and the self-discovery it created. Connecting to what I loved to do physically changed me. As I stepped into what brought me joy, something began to shift, not just on the inside but on the outside too. I didn't notice it right away, but others did. When friends came from Canada to visit, their first comment wasn't about the weather or how long it had been; it was, "You look so different, Susan!" And they were right. I was connected to my passion and felt that I had a purpose that aligned with my core values.

The needs of my normal self were met; I was connected to my church community and the community at large, and I was given the opportunity to connect to knowledge outside the church, which was something I had wanted to do for many years. And I was able to make goals and fulfill them in a way that made me more strongly connected to those around me. My spiritual self shifted away from fearing those over me, even though I would flush with heat every time someone asked me about dance, and I began to believe that God wanted me to start to minister again, both in church and outside of the four walls. After all, it was about spheres of influence and mountains to climb. Within months, I was asked to be on various teams. I accepted, not as a "headliner," but as someone passionate about the ministry. Life was moving forward. It was more than moving forward, I was flourishing. It was evident in me, just as it would also be evident in anyone. "Hey, thank you," I said. "God really has done amazing things in our lives," giving all the hard-won work to God.

Purpose is the thread that connects the dots to everything you do that leads you to an extraordinary life.

—Oprah

26

TEAM EFFORT

There is no *I* in team.

Upon securing the rights to the Heroes program in the US, we knew it would require a team effort. Our long-time friends Debra and Gary loved the idea and they wanted to be part of it. We were beyond thrilled. Debra and Gary invested their time, money, vision, and energy into the business, and together, we gathered a team of leaders in their respective industries—church, education, and business—to begin training as facilitators in the material. Yet again, in this next business adventure, we hadn't learned to consult lawyers.

John Henry and I met with business representatives as prospective investors, and I excelled in my role to explain how the program worked. A comment kept coming up: "When you have something like this for adults, come back and we'll for sure invest." However, since our program focused so heavily on schools and youth, most companies were not able to invest. As I received the feedback, it was both encouraging and challenging. I remember thinking, "One day, we'll need to create an adult program." It wasn't a setback, just a nudge towards growth and possibilities.

Alongside growing interest in the Heroes program, our connections within a particular school system led to a training program for teachers, and I was chosen to coordinate it. *Lucky me!* I flourished in this role. Everything was set and ready to go. The training for the teachers went very well, and at this particular school, we had both the principal and school counsellor as facilitators, so their involvement brought a unique strength and credibility to the program.

I walked across the entryway and was greeted by the school counsellor who asked me to come to the principal's office. Jokingly, I said, "Am I in trouble?" The short answer was yes. As I stepped into the principal's office, I was told that the program was cancelled before it even had the chance to start. "Unfortunately, it's politics," I was told. The principal, school counsellor, and teachers were on board, but somewhere at the district level, there were differing opinions. I wondered if it was because it was a Canadian program rather than a US-born program. Either way, I could both see and hear the disappointment in the principal's and counsellor's voices. Their faces reflected the frustration of something being shut down by forces beyond their control. It was a heavy moment, the weight of lost opportunity filled the air.

As I drove home that day, I pulled over and stopped my vehicle by the side of the road and purposely got out to shake the dust off my feet. Speaking into the air, "We have great starts—but." Time was passing and so was our ability to move forward. We were falling short of our timeline and falling short meant getting short on finances. In the end, and after a-year-and-a-half-long process, we were low on resources.

I wasn't sure why, but I felt like Humpy Dumpty who fell off the wall. Something wasn't right, but I didn't know what. Where was the God of breakthrough? Why did it seem like we were always in a breakdown? And why did it seem that God, in the end, would always elude me. I experienced triggering intrusive memories and images of my conversation with God as a young girl in the backseat of my mum's car when I asked Him why He hated me. Questions that sprouted like wildflowers in the field of my mind, yet I always returned to the thought, questioning myself if there was something inherently wrong between God and me. This living in extremes was draining all my resources—emotionally, mentally, and physically. This breaker anointing continued to elude me.

This time when our business failed, I was not only exhausted, I was becoming disenfranchised. A prayer meeting was called to help us seek God's direction on our behalf and only one other couple showed up. It wasn't just this meeting or my imagination. More and more, I found myself caught in the same cycle, one moment part of the "in group," and the next, I was pushed to the fringes. It was a pattern that kept repeating, leaving me feeling both seen and unseen, included and isolated, sometimes hopeful, sometimes shut out. It was that push-pull that happens in unhealthy groups. This time, our marriage was being talked about among other couples. I knew because one of those couples trusted me enough to tell me. I tried not to be discouraged, but that familiar feeling of otherness seemed to wrap itself around me and I began to detach from church.

Deciding to create some distance between me and the church was a blessing in disguise. As I stepped back and gave myself space, I began to notice patterns I hadn't seen before: dynamics and unspoken expectations that had been difficult to recognize up close. Stepping back from church also didn't just bring clarity, it also shed light on patterns in my marriage too. Patterns that kept recycling, church after church, season after season, no matter what country we lived in.

My father had fallen and broken his hip. With his existing diagnosis of dementia, there was concern about whether or not he'd recover. "God, please let me be there when my dad transitions. He still doesn't know you and I really need one last opportunity to minister to him," I prayed. My prayer was quickly answered; a friend gifted me a flight voucher to return to Canada to see my father and I was able to be with Dad when it mattered most. I had the chance to pray over him and tell him of how much he was loved.

Upon returning stateside, our mentor and friend, Grant, lost the battle to brain cancer, but love still won in the end. Grant was deeply respected and loved both within and outside the church. His love was simple, yet profound—if you were human, you had value. That's just how Grant loved people. Love Wins was his motto, and he had a tattoo to prove it.

With both my father's and Grant's passing, I was beginning to feel something I hadn't felt in years. Despair was rising. I was caught up as catastrophic thinking and spiritual trauma spun a dark web during a time of great loss. Yet, the only question I could muster was, "What do I need to do to get our breakthrough!" Remember the prophetic word:

You will go through many things that would seem dire, desperate, but the Lord is training you to rise up in the anointing he has placed in you.

I was desperate and I was exhausted—completely caught in survival mode. One might think that I was done. But I wasn't …

When you are tempted to give up, your breakthrough is probably just around the corner.

—Joyce Meyer

Part Three

$\overline{\underline{27}}$

FULL CIRCLE

My full circle began in 2011 with the decision to return to Canada. I had received some money that my father left me, which gave me the resources I needed to make decisions and act on them. Returning to Canada wasn't an easy choice; during our five years living stateside, I had found my place in our community and I saw both my children excel in sports, pursue their own passions, and find hope for the future. I had come to love many aspects of where we lived, such as our home, friends, and church. I had built a life that was hard to let go of. Yet, the fact that I had never been able to secure a green card left me financially dependent on John Henry, and because he needed to apply for a visa each time he worked for another company, the risks outweighed my desire to remain—especially as our son was nearing graduation. The pressure of finding our next source of income was too much. The never-ending cycle of which bill to pay and which bill could wait made me look for a more secure future for my children. As Canadian citizens, that secure future was back in our home country. Yet, every time I spoke about returning to Canada, tears would unexpectedly well up and I'd find myself apologizing for them. Each time I shared my decision to return to Canada with friends at church, I would have to steady myself as my voice quivered: "Yes, we're returning to Canada. It's the right decision for our future," was often followed by, "I'm so sorry, I don't know why I'm crying," as I would wipe away my tears.

This one decision, as uncertain as it was, changed the course of our lives. First, I transitioned our son, Ben, and then I transitioned our daughter, Abigail. We would land on Vancouver Island where we lived with Katheryn and Mike, long-time friends who had become chosen family. I didn't have the funds to rent a home for my family over the long term, so this would be a safe and supportive landing spot to begin to start over. We landed with suitcases in hand and began resettling into life on the Island, recalibrating our priorities and restarting our lives from the ground up.

John Henry remained in the US, believing there were more opportunities there for employment, but within that same year, he joined us on the Island. Through conversations over the phone, countries apart, John Henry miraculously found employment in Victoria, and we tried to begin again. We moved into our rented home and each of us focused on rebuilding rather than reconnecting, and so our toxic relationship cycle continued. We focused on life for our children and getting them acclimatized. During this time, my inheritance was being used to resettle, reestablish, and rebuild our lives. Unfortunately, the work that John Henry had secured on the Island did not turn out as promised. Life was getting more and more complicated, and so I found myself questioning everything once again. What compounded the self-doubt was the fact that I was the one who made the decision to return to Canada, as John Henry had asked me to stay in the US, but I thought I was hearing God tell me to return to Canada. This "tough transition" made me wonder again if I had ever heard God at all.

All my energy was spent on my children and my work. I found work at a chiropractic clinic and very quickly felt at home. In many ways, working in the holistic field felt similar to my experience in church. My workplace offered a sense of community that could rival any congregation; their focus was on transforming lives, guiding people from pain to health. There was an undeniable energy in the atmosphere, one that sparked hope and healing. Almost immediately, I had somewhere to belong—my normal self knew how to create connection and community. Here I was, building relationships without being driven by the fear of my spiritual self.

My role as a decompression technician allowed me to engage deeply in meaningful work and find a new sense of purpose. The clinic provided a space for me to introduce the Life Languages communication profile I had been certified in and I was given opportunities to speak, share, present, and help build both culture and community. I was able to connect with people and their stories, as many patients would come for multiple treatments per week. I found myself connecting to the patients and my gifts emerged naturally. My intuition sharpened and my knowledge of self deepened as I attuned to the healing environment. I didn't think of it as surviving; to me, it felt like I was truly living. Working at the clinic gave me a sense of vitality. Getting to work in an environment that facilitated transformed lives and hope did the same work within me as I had experienced with prophecy, minus the toxic spirituality. Work became my happy place.

For six years, John Henry and I continued to cycle through well-set patterns in our marriage. I was working for an hourly wage, but that didn't matter to me. What I was attaching to was so much more valuable. I was existing in my normal self—I just didn't know it yet.

Loving what you do is the secret to everything.

—Julia Roberts

28

UNHOOKING VELCRO KISSES

When I returned to Canada, I sought out a church that had the same flavour and energy as I had experienced in Valparaiso—I especially sought out churches that were linked to Bethel Redding and Global Legacy. Each church I attended seemed to be missing that special sauce. The churches seemed dry, behind, and even boring; until, that is, I found New Life Church in Kelowna. My mum and her husband lived just outside of Kelowna in Lake Country, and each time I visited them, I met with a long-time friend, Gabriella, who I had met on a trip to Kelowna just prior to moving stateside. Gabriella had a connection with New Life Church, and she knew the leadership there very well. Whenever I was in town, Gabriella and I would attend church together and then spend hours at Starbucks retracing what God had been doing in our lives. I found myself wishing I could move there so I could plug into this church and this relationship with Gabriella; I missed the spiritually charged atmosphere.

In between my visits, I allowed myself to become curious about the energetics that I saw both in Christian communities and in the holistic field I was working in. In the holistic context, energetics refers to the movement, flow, and quality of subtle energy—vibration, frequency, etc. In Christianity, *energy* isn't usually the word used, but many believers describe the felt sense of the Holy Spirit—warmth, tingling, peace, power, or presence—which functions much like an energetic experience. As Oprah would say, "everything is energy," and I was beginning to see the truth in that.

For one of our clinic's team-building events, almost the entire team made their way to Seattle to attend a chiropractor conference with the doctors. Two days of meetings. It reminded me in many ways of a church conference: the speakers, the breakouts, the book tables. I realized that I had been so immersed in church that I had only attended church conferences and homeschooling conferences. I was excited and ready to be there.

It was at this chiropractic conference that I had my first encounter with Dr. Joe Dispenza. I was introduced to Dr. Joe through a video series that we would watch at the clinic during our Monday morning team development times. We were fortunate enough that the chiropractors, who were also the owners, shared their knowledge and resources with us. Watching the videos, I clearly remember the effect his words had on me. "You think 60,000 to 70,000 thoughts every single day, and 90% of those thoughts are the same thoughts as the day before," Dr. Joe says from the stage on the TV screen. If you googled Dr. Joe, you'd quickly find one of his main messages: In order to change your life and create lasting change, you need to change your thoughts, and that an individual needs to become aware of their unconscious thought patterns and actively choose to think differently. Today, Dr. Joe Dispenza's name is synonymous with thought. After hearing him speak at the conference, there was a lunch break. Most of our team went to lunch, but I went to Dr. Joe's table. He was right there in front of me and my mind went blank. I just stared.

A few years later, I used Dr. Joe's words as I introduced a segment at a conference with the doctors from the clinic.

On stage at the Victoria Convention Centre at the Empress Hotel, I spoke about the impact of thoughts, feelings, and how they can create a state in our bodies and brains. I spoke about how to interrupt and create a new state. I led the participants through an exercise that was both visual and practical. And when I was finished, the next doctor took the stage and brought their piece of the session. It was moments like these that connected me back to my normal self, where I taught, helped others, and set goals and attained them.

When I chose to recertify with Life Languages in 2014, I presented the profile to the clinic, and it was so successful that I was granted the opportunity to utilize it within the clinic's existing business. The doctors even helped me make connections with other business owners. This was all connecting me back to an empowered state of being—back to the Susan who had made the decision to return to Canada. Yet, nothing was changing in my marriage—it was only getting into a more well-worn rut. Without help, without being willing to seek outside help, we were doomed to fail.

My first search for professional help led me to a website that listed numerous counsellors local to me. I read each bio, their specialities, their qualifications, and I studied their pictures. I chose a counsellor who was a licenced social worker, who had over fifteen years of experience. Her face was kind and inviting, and her bio spoke about how your past can inform your present, but it does not have to define you. I wanted that: a new definition of who I was in the world outside of the church. I was feeling empowered but also torn. I still hadn't realized that I was existing through two selves.

I began counselling. My first session was in her home. I sat in the driveway praying for protection, for insight, and for hope. Yes, you read that correctly. I prayed for protection because this was the first person, the first woman, the first counsellor—I'll call her Denise—who I was giving myself permission to speak to outside of the influence of the church. I wish I could give you a play-by-play scene of our first meeting, but I don't fully remember what we talked about. What I do remember was the feeling of hope at the possibility of creating a future that wasn't hindered by my past—the feeling that I as a woman, with or without my husband, could move forward in life, and especially that I could trust someone's counsel and knowledge outside of the church. I felt as though I could breathe all the way to my toes.

What we focused on at first was understanding the difference between *fusion* and *differentiation*, which are terms taken from the Bowen Family Systems Theory. Learning and understanding about the significance of emotional fusion and differentiation in relationships was foundational. We talked about the difference between enmeshment and boundaries and that enmeshment could be emotional or physical. She taught me about moving from a state of dependency to independence and individuation and to avoid the unhealthy blurring of boundaries, which causes a loss of individuality and impedes the creation of, and in my case, the retention of one's sense of self while being connected to others. I hadn't realized how much of my self was given away in order to fit in.

Since my initial attachment trauma happened in childhood, connection meant survival. When I understood this, I could see that it was right and good for me not to give myself away, but to hold onto myself, my wants, my needs (which is also being differentiated) while I was connected to others. I also realized clearly that I was empathic. I could read a room before I even entered it. I can feel other people's feelings, whether I wanted to or not. In church, that sense was often misinterpreted as spiritual discernment, when it was just emotions being felt in a meeting. Emotions are contagious. Have you ever got yourself caught up at a music concert or sports game? Pay attention to how you feel before you go into that concert or sporting event and compare that to how you feel afterwards—you might see that you leave changed (or at least influenced by the atmosphere), sometimes even on a emotional high. All those years I had spent in spiritual climates, in intercession, and in extended worship crafted a highly sensitive emotional/spiritual attunement to the environments that I was in, and not necessarily in a good way. Being so open and sensitive could make travel tricky, as I had learned to tap in energetically to not just people but to regions.

By developing emotional differentiation, I could begin to unhook myself from environmental overtones and see what was me and what was the person or the environment. Learning these life skills allowed me to not only manage my emotions better, but I could begin to communicate more effectively; I was no longer enmeshed in the emotions of everyone in the room, or felt the need to manage unhealthy relationships. Doing this eventually led me to learn to make decisions independent of others and it fostered healthier and more authentic relationships.

I was moving out of dependency and fostering independence for the first time in my adult life—doing something in my fifties that developmentally is typically done in your twenties. In healthy normal childhood development, dependent/independent to interdependent is a healthy developmental process. Because of my trauma bond to prophecy and waiting for the end of the world to happen (subconsciously, of course) and the trauma I experienced entering young adulthood, I was left to believe that I was not safe on my own. I believed that my survival depended on being connected to someone who could protect me. It was a child state, a dependent state. Connection was misinterpreted in my brain and body as enmeshment. Learning healthy independence was another way to unhook myself from those Velcro Kisses.

After the first three years of working with Denise, she had become a source of strength in my life, and she asked me if I had heard about the book *Educated* when it was first published in 2018. She was reading it and thought of me, saying I might be interested in reading it. As I mentioned in the introduction, Tara's book was the first story that I heard where the person didn't spiritually bypass apocalyptic thinking or messaging. What struck me in Tara's account was that when she was at university, she would find herself sleepwalking and waking up screaming in the streets or staying in bed all day. I was both comforted and mortified reading the account of her story, but ultimately encouraged. The next time I encountered the book *Educated* was the day I was walking into my second lawyer's office. This time, I was empowered with courage, and I also had another friend beside me as I signed the papers to start my divorce.

The first time I walked into a lawyer's office, I was in a "leaving" state of the marriage cycle—I was housesitting for my friend Katheryn, but I was ahead of myself. What I wanted wasn't solidified internally. John Henry and I were still stuck in the same pattern: stay, go, restart, leave, and return. Sitting across from my first lawyer trying to explain where and why I was at in life emotionally, financially, and relationally, my face and body flooded with shame as I tried to find the words. I felt so much shame. Trying to explain something that was so complex felt as if I was trying to separate thousands of little threads that had become so knotted and tangled up that trying to define my situation only made the knots tighter and more difficult to undo. Now here I was, two years later, once again walking into another lawyer's office; I chose a woman this time, and I had more language, more understanding of relationships, and more clarity of why I stayed, then left, only to restart, then leave, and return. The book on the legal aid's desk caught my attention—it was *Educated*.

When I sat down to share my story this time, I mentioned that it was a little bit like the author's in the book *Educated*; I too believed in the impeding apocalypse, except that was fifty years ago. Tara still had a lot of years in front of her. As it turns out, the female lawyer sitting across the desk from me also had relatives who believed in the Rapture. We had a common ground. I let out the breath I was trying to talk through, and tears fell freely as I began to share how I came to be in that chair. Unhooking Velcro: another hook and loop undone.

We are all of us more complicated than the roles we are assigned in the stories other people tell.

—Tara Westover

29

LEARNING TO QUESTION

In 2018, I crossed paths again with my now husband, Andrew. I first met Andrew in 2012 when he was a patient at the clinic that I worked at. "Hi, I don't think we've met," I said as I took his hand and introduced myself, "my name is Susan." "Hello, Susan, my name is Andrew. Nice to meet you." To which I responded, "Anything new or different since your last visit?" Andrew often has people in stitches as he shares how we first met. I was so matter of fact, a professional and very much married.

At that time, I was working in the decompression area. Patients would come into our section of the clinic—we had about ten to twelve decompression tables—and as a technician, it was my job to prep the table and assess the patients prior to their treatment. Often, there was room for health coaching, spinal health coaching, or personal connection that fostered a sense of community. Some patients would come back two or more times per week. This is how Andrew and I first met.

Fast forward six years—I was still working in the decompression area and Andrew returned to the clinic, and as it happened, I was separated. I never thought much about Andrew, other than the fact that he was one of those patients that everyone in decompression enjoyed seeing. The last time I spoke to Andrew before he asked me out, he came in for his decompression treatment and said something that I thought was uncalled for and I told him just that, politely and professionally (see how far I've come). So, when Andrew came in for his next treatment, I happened to be at the desk area and upon greeting me, he offered an apology for what he said. Imagine my surprise when he leaned over to ask me out as he was leaving. I was so surprised that I physically left the floor and went into the doctor's office, and with one look at my face, the doctor asked, "What just happened to you!?" and thus began our love story.

I am of the generation who follows protocol and upon receiving multiple yeses, Andrew and I began our relationship first through email, then we graduated to texting, and so when we went on our first date late that fall—my first date after twenty-seven years of marriage—I felt as though I already knew the man who pulled the chair out for me to take my seat. And taking that seat led to our first kiss and so on. But it was not long after that first date when I knew that I had to tell Andrew my story. If I wanted a full heart-to-heart connection, I couldn't keep secrets, and better for him to know sooner rather than later. I knew all too well how that felt.

One night, while we were sitting on the floor by his fireplace with the charcuterie board I had made for us, I said, "Andrew, there are some things I think you should know about me. I need to tell you about where I come from. I think you should know because I wouldn't want to have you find out after we fall in love. I've had information withheld from me in past relationships and I don't want that in ours." Andrew could see the concerned look on my face and we both felt the surge of sadness before I even said a word. And with that, I began to tell Andrew about my childhood, about a life always worried about the end of the world, about the life I felt was stolen from me, and what that created. Feeling isolated most of my life, out of step and out of rhythm with the world around me, and the shame that I felt for not having more to bring to a relationship than just myself, especially now at my age. Andrew listened intently and then he paused and said, "You should write about this; people need to hear your story. The courage you have to do what you've done, that's amazing." In all honesty, I was braced for what he could have said. I didn't expect to be met with kindness and compassion. My story was embraced—what I had weathered through had been validated rather than received with unsolicited advice or worse. Unhooking Velcro: another hook and loop undone.

Andrew asked me two questions: How did I survive, and how did I get out?

Looking back, I didn't see it as survival—I saw it as my life. Through working with Denise, I was finally able to explain that I had compartmentalized my normal self and spiritual self; it wasn't until I started to reconnect the two when I was back in Canada that the tug-of-war inside of me became apparent. In all honesty, I never thought of myself as surviving except for the fact that I always seemed to be looking for my breakthrough in the form of getting *enough* or reaching the right *when*. *Enough* always seemed just out of reach and *when* seemed to be down the road, whether that be financial stability, or stability period. *When* seemed to be something to wait for, a perpetual "not yet." I relied on the kindness of long-time friendships, physically and emotionally, not realizing one day I would need to face reality. I focused my time and attended to what I could do rather than what I couldn't. I focused on my family and finding work that aligned with my values.

The second question wasn't as easy to answer, because I never had that one clear moment where I said, "That's it—I'm done, I'm out." I did share that when I initially came out of the NAR, it was incredibly difficult to make even the simplest of decisions. I was so used to deferring to God or to prophets. The Elijah List was a staple in my morning routine, a daily read. Then, I learned about a concept called priming. Priming can be likened to mental preparation. Something you see, hear, or experience that plants a seed in your mind that makes you more likely to think, feel, or act in a certain way afterward. It's part of influence. It happens more often than we realize. Our mind is being nudged in a direction before we even notice that it's moving. It's easy to spot it in advertising—it might be less easy to spot in your local church or in your daily horoscope.

Taking back my life meant taking back my mind. From the simple decisions to the clothes I wore, the type of cheese I bought, and the vehicle I drove, everything was filtered through spiritual lenses. Tones and certain kinds of music would cause flashbacks—both visual and emotional. I was asked on many occasions, "Susan, where did you go?" But I was sitting right next to the person asking. I had to activate my capacity for critical thought and learn to become a wise consumer rather than make decisions purely from an emotional charge.

In his book, *Combating Cult Mind Control*, Stephen Hassan writes about the ways people leave cults. Given my experience leaving the church, I would agree with his conclusions. He groups people who have left cults or groups of undue influence into three categories. The first are those he calls walk-outs, which tend to be the largest number of people. Walk-outs are people who leave a cult *on their own*, without structured help, intervention, or counselling. These are the people where they come to a moment of clarity, or frustration, or even an event that cause them to say "That's it, I'm out." In my opinion, those who walk out leave with a sense of agency. The second are those who are kicked out, often in a burned-out condition, both psychologically and physically. They might leave with feelings of betrayal or shame, and may have less agency over timing or the terms of their exit. Thirdly, there are those who are counselled out, who are given information that causes them to leave. These are the individuals who exit might be supported intentionally, maybe by family or friends, professionals, or by someone guiding them through the process. Someone who is counselled out can still face resistance (from self, or from those inside the group) and can have lingering trauma, though the recovery process might be smoother with support. I see myself in the counselled-out category.

Counselling, for me, takes on many forms; it's about getting missing information that educates, links experiences and emotions, defines problems, labels trauma, and fosters health. It's important that education isn't wrapped in spiritual language and is focused on social influence, mind control—and the many different forms that can take—child development, attachment styles, and how the brain processes information. It's about connecting to people and spaces that are safe and free from undue influence or personal agendas. It's about places where stories can be shared and people can mirror back your truth with grace and humanity. Counselling, for me, was not always about someone leading me through a process; it was about creating a safe space to begin to understand my situation and come to my own conclusions. Far too long, many who come out of religious and spiritual backgrounds have been told what to think, what to do, and how to be. I am convinced that we are born with an innate knowing that, if allowed, will guide us better than any ideology or system of belief.

Through creating a safe space with Denise, I was able to start to deal with the compartmentalizing I had been living with. When I first attempted to reconnect to the part of me that I call my normal self, people began to notice changes within me. As my normal self, I presented as a strong-willed person; I was clear-headed, sharper, more alive. This is when the tug-of-war came to the front. I would go for a counselling session with Denise and would return self-directed and with strong emotional boundaries. Then, it would wear off, and I would begin to wobble again. For reasons I don't recall, I reached out for a few coaching sessions with a coach from Bethel Redding. The woman who became my coach was the wife of a minister—her husband ran a ministry that was focused on heart-centred coaching through the lens of Jesus. There were many spiritual questions that Denise didn't have the bandwidth for; one of my main questions was about if I had "permission" to leave my marriage, especially since there wasn't any adultery. After all, I believed we had made a covenant when we said our marriage vows in front of the two pastors, the people present, and God. During those coaching sessions, the woman would lead me through a spiritual template of questions, visions, and answers, and she always used

Jesus or the Bible as the "source." After those coaching calls, my friend Katheryn told me that she could see I was deeply conflicted and was questioning my life, my stance, and my new-found perspective. This tug-of-war went on for a few months, and I would even find myself pleading my then husband to give it another try. Not just because my word was my bond, but also because my heart always wanted family first. I didn't understand this to be a trauma point in my life nor did I know what cognitive dissonance was. The fact was that even though my heart may have always wanted family first, the reality was we were not a family and hadn't been one for many years. We simply coexisted.

To Andrew's question about how I got out, I would say this tug-of-war period was pivotal because I learned so many new perspectives that helped me understand my normal self and my spiritual self. I learned about the brain, the energy of the nervous system, the felt flow of somatics, and the energy of the heart. This all drew me in and began to make sense in a way that seemed both ancient and deeply personal and gradually became the lenses through which I began to see life. Time and time again, the uncanny coincidences I encountered in church happened at work: People who worked closely together would often show up dressed in the same colour tones without planning it. It became our new normal—joking about who got the memo and who didn't. In church, we'd say, "Who was picking up what the Spirit was saying and who wasn't?" At times, a patient's name would come up in conversation, and almost like clockwork, they would show up at the clinic days later. When I was in church, we would pray about someone in our congregation who came to mind and they'd show up or reach out soon after. These experiences only piqued my curiosity, and I gave myself permission to step into territory that once was forbidden in the church. Asking all these questions and following my curiosity all began to undue the hooks and loops that I had been attached to.

I gave myself permission to ask all kinds of questions and to follow curiosity—that's how I began to find my way out. This was my new beginning. I had conversations about everything I was learning with people both in and out of the church. I didn't throw the baby out with the bath water; I held onto the concepts that felt real in both worlds, while beginning to challenge just about everything else.

Asking questions is the first way to begin change.

NOW WHAT?

Do I go to church today? No. Will I go to church again? Likely not. Do I still believe in God? Yes, but not in the same way I used to. I believe there is a power, an energy, and a mystery, if you will, that still exists. I have reverence for something larger than myself. I believe in moments of grace; I believe in synchronicity that may feel like magical moments. I no longer put Christianese terms to them. What I have come to value more than a black-and-white decision regarding if there is a God or not is the asking if there is love or not. And I have not found love in indoctrination. I found more agendas there.

I do believe that prophecy and seeking breakthroughs are both powerful and can be easily manipulative, especially for people in vulnerable places in their lives, like a season of transition, a season of loss, illness, a move to a new city, entering secondary education away from home, a divorce or breakup, or if they have holes in their attachment processes. In my own life, I have come to see that my childhood loneliness and lack of support at pivotal points in my development created vulnerabilities that blinded me to my unhealthy relationships. Numerous times, I have both read and heard stories about people being taken in and hoodwinked when they thought it couldn't happen to them. Yet, it did. Personally, I don't believe anyone is immune to these types of things; the more you don't think it can happen to you, the more likely that it will.

Prophetic atmospheres are highly contagious. Emotions run high, and social bonding is powerful. Having someone share details of your life that you thought only God knew is powerfully seductive, unless, of course, they've researched your social media. I've seen and experienced the power of the collective. Synergy is real. Trance states happen and are encouraged in the churches I've been a part of; in my opinion they just call it "living the supernatural lifestyle." If you were to ask me about energetics, I would have to say yes, I still believe in energetics even if it can be a hot topic. My son Ben and I have lots of discussions about energetics, and he's got some good points. When I speak of energetics, I think of the study or awareness of how energy moves, changes, and affects us—not just in physics or biology, but in daily life. It's the *felt sense* of how people, environments, emotions, and intentions carry a kind of charge that influences our mood, motivation, and well-being.

The other ways I've experienced energetics I do not have an explanation for—yet. I have read the cult experts' materials and listened to podcasts, and I still have questions. I have seen those who have given their lives to the supernatural realm share testimony about the cost of their anointing. One prophet in particular shared about how he went too far in the Spirit and what it cost him. I have watched prophet after prophet bring revelations, breakthroughs, and movements, and years later read about the abuse they'd inflicted upon others. It's often those who trusted and followed them that become victims. Some of these high-profile and long-time apostles and prophets are banned from ministry today, while others believe they have had another visitation from God to relaunch their ministries, and so they did.

In my opinion, if you compared a guru and some Christian prophets side by side, we might just see that there is a lot of overlap. Especially if we looked at the trail that they left in their wake, I believe we'd come to notice that, just like the recovery groups I have been a part of, a lot of the signs and symptoms are the same. But that is my opinion. We each must choose what we believe.

So, where am I today? I'd say let's backtrack a bit and talk about something no prophet saw coming: the pandemic. The arrival of the COVID-19 pandemic, to my brain and body, was more than a global health crisis, it signaled "the end." Subconsciously, the pandemic awakened unresolved religious and spiritual trauma that set off alarm bells to my spiritual self. It unearthed rooted fears that I had thought I had already weeded out. COVID, for me, wasn't just about trying to stay safe; it was about trying to keep my balance. I did just enough religious trauma work to get through the initial pandemic, but as the pandemic lingered, and uncertainty grew, and alongside the rise of conspiracy theories, my anxiety increased and it triggered panic attacks. I would end up having multiple heart procedures in an attempt to ablate hot spots in my heart that triggered paroxysmal atrial fibrillation. All these things added to the tug-of-war and that push-pull in my life and body. My ability to put on my professional face was slipping as my trauma became harder to hide. For me, this is where my grit became my godsend.

I have always been a seeker, so I used that to become a lifelong educated learner. I knew there were answers, I just needed to keep digging until I found them. I would come to find those who were credentialed and experienced in their field rather than talking to well-meaning people who were further ahead of me in life, who wanted to offer help, but they tended to see my situation through the lens of their life, which didn't help. I needed a trauma-sensitive and informed perspective. A year into the pandemic, I found groups of people who had come out of religious and spiritual abuse, coercive control, undue influence, or cultic groups. I saw immediately that we may have had different experiences, but the majority of us had the same symptoms and were searching for similar answers. We looked to those who specialized in the field of undue influence, cults, and coercion. I've already mentioned Steven Hassan, and here I will add names such as Rachael Bernstein and her podcast *Indoctrination* and Jania Lalich and her book *Take Back Your Life*. I found Dr. John Hunter's work on the dopamine hypothesis very relevant as well as his book *Manufacturing Mania*. In the groups I connected to, we began to identify and use language that describes the importance of needing to *deconstruct* or *unravel*, if you prefer a gentler word. Deconstructing our beliefs or unravelling all those threads that were so tightly woven together made for precision work, and complexity takes time to unravel. For me, this meant unravelling the threads of long-held beliefs, beliefs that had bonded me to prophecy. Each of these threads also bonded me to relationships that were unstable, unsafe, and top heavy. Giving myself the time and space I needed to tease apart each thread to see where it would lead, I stopped when I needed to stop and listened to my body. Often, my mind wanted to keep going to find the answer to its many questions, but my nervous system said stop. And so, I did. I learned about rhythm and its importance to the nervous system and to the brain. I embraced the significance of rest and worked to slow my pace. Keeping in mind the parable of The Tortoise and the Hare, I slowly but consistently learned to let go of what no longer served me, even if that meant relationships that became outdated or a way of thinking that needed to evolve and grow.

Today, I have found that I have many happy places, not just one. I love digging through thrift stores for hidden finds, walking by the sea, trying new recipes, and having deep talks with my son. I dive into conversations with my daughter about how young women navigate life in today's world, enjoy a glass of good wine, say yes to adventures, and cherish time with my favourite people. I spend hours researching topics that spark my curiosity, grounding myself with my feet in the sand or cool grass—feeling alive and present—and I purposely choose to swim without being tied to my Apple Watch; choosing these things allows me to make room for unmanufactured moments in my life. At one pivot point, I stopped focusing on the influencers and started looking for what was authentic, real, and lasting.

Today, I stopped identifying love with loyalty and like with happy. People can love but they might not have the capacity to be steady. Love is an emotion, but loyalty is a choice. People can stay out of duty, history, or principle, but it might not contain heart. That's undue loyalty. I can only choose loyalty from an unbounded choice; it can't be forced. Like is about preference; it points outward, as in "I like Indian food, I like ice cream," and, most importantly, it can change. Happy is an emotion, a state of being, if you will—it points inward. Neither of these relate to loyalty. I'm going to choose more of what fosters my inner sense of happiness and peace, because love is from the heart and I want my life to be centred around my heart and balanced with my brain.

Doing this allowed me to create more alignment with what is valuable to me today. As I'm in the phase of reclaiming and rebuilding my life, an easy metaphor for my life right now is that of building a home. I link this metaphor to my new, emerging self. My home has levels in it—yes, I do still love levels. The foundation is where I ground myself in my values that keep me steady—my values steady my heart and remind me what truly matters in this life. This is also where I connect to and integrate my emotional and relational worlds. It's where I journal, go for a walk, take a bath, or go for a swim, anything that is grounding for me. Integration is key. Then, the main floor represents my daily life and habits that support who I am becoming. On the main floor (my daily life) is where I add lots of new furniture, which can be one new practice, skill, or routine—whatever makes my new life real and lived in. I might join a class, meet a friend for coffee, throw a dinner party, or even change up my morning routine. Then, I have an upper floor where I let myself dream, create, and allow my spiritual practice to grow. Moving through each level, I remind myself that life is a journey. For me, it's been a journey integrating my spiritual self and my normal self. This metaphor creates a quiet homecoming, where the past no longer holds power over me, only perspective. In my new home, healing is now about reclaiming all the things that belong to me.

Your energy is your most expensive currency. And not everyone can afford it.

—Déjà Rae, *Come Home to Yourself*

FINALLY HOME

As you can see, my process wasn't linear. At times, it felt slow, other times, it felt intense—especially during my season of learning to roll. Experiencing one fall that resulted in a plate and screws in my wrist was one thing, but falling again months later and experiencing a fractured hip was another thing altogether, especially when it turned out to be a malunion. I used that physical pain to dive into my emotional pain, and I leaned into my writing to help me process everything. Doing this work, I began to trust myself, and as I did that, I began to take back authorship over my own narrative, connecting the dots of my story as I gently pulled each thread. This book has shown those threads around my childhood trauma, my trauma bond to prophecy, and my unhealthy attachment to people and groups. Now, integration has been the key to stopping the tug-of-war between my normal self and my spiritual self.

Integration at its core means bringing parts together to form a whole. It's about unity without losing uniqueness; the parts still matter, but together, they create something greater. For me, my first experience of integration happened during an EMDR session. EMDR is a type of therapy that helps people deal with emotions and memories associated with past trauma. I remember the surprise I felt as I watched my two selves merge. My response was notable. I named the integration of my normal self and my spiritual self *Uniquely Susan*. I felt different; I homed in on the sensation of strength in my body, and I realized that resiliency got me back on my feet, but integration gave me the ability to see more clearly.

Before I go any further, I want to make it clear that EMDR is not the solution for everyone. Nor am I a therapist. I have also spent much time dissecting and understanding my traumas from a cognitive perspective, labeling, identifying, and understanding them cognitively before trying to deal with the emotions of my traumas. One thing that kept me stuck was trying to emotionally process my experiences without having the words or language to describe those emotions. Also, with my years of experience in ministry, self-awareness was not something I needed to learn. Many of us who come out of these environments are overly self-aware. Putting the focus outside of ourselves is more often the challenge.

In my experience, EMDR helped me process memories that were stuck or locked in my brain. This type of therapy helped me to emotionally regulate my nervous system. I no longer was constantly triggered when I read the news or heard another conspiracy theory or the latest COVID debate. I began to know in my brain and in my body that COVID was not "the end." These are all Velcro Kisses in my life that needed to be unhooked. Not acknowledging my experience, my brain was stuck in survival mode. Acting as if I was okay and trying to put on my professional face, my brain acted as if the threat was still present and it was exhausting. As I processed through EMDR, my brain was able to form new neural pathways, which is important because it wasn't just about reintegrating memories but also making new connections, which allowed me to see clearer and think better.

Through integration, I was able to bring together my normal self—which was based on family, connection, community, and attaining goals to create a future for myself—and my spiritual self—which was based on God, fear, and surviving the future. Today, I can tell you my story without that emotional charge that comes with being triggered. The first letter to little me in this book came from one of my EMDR processing sessions. I chose to share this experience because it touched me deeply, it was both healing and fascinating to realize that, even as an adult woman, I could return to and resource my inner child.

I noticed that my values became clearer and stronger, which has resulted in more self-confidence. I felt myself standing strong again. This is all part of what I call learning to roll. Doing this work created edges that were round rather than pointed. And round edges allowed me to roll and gain the momentum to get back up again, this time working with my natural resilience rather than fighting against it.

Today, I navigate my life through my values, allowing them to ground me rather than by goals as I did when I was waiting for "the end." Attempting to see how far I could get, I realized I was trying to accomplish "it" rather than create my life from things that mattered most. Rebalance was about integrating both my normal self and my spiritual self. Realizing that it didn't have to be one or the other, it wasn't a battle about which self would win. There never needed to be a tug-of-war. There needed to be integration.

When I broke my wrist in 2023, I had recently left the clinic that I had been working at for over 10 years. At a subconscious level, my thoughts kept trying to figure out why I was spinning rather than moving forward with my life. Why did I feel like I just left Pineridge Church all over again? After all, it was a working relationship rather than a church community. In tracing that one thread all the way back to how I attached to communities and to groups, it made complete sense why I would template my life to my workplace in the same way I had learned to attached to groups and church communities. It was still through the lens of fitting and belonging. I have learned from Dr. Diane Poole Heller and her work on attachments styles that we are born with the innate ability to create secure attachment styles. I like this perspective. Learning that attachment styles can change from person to person and environment to environment, I could see this at play in my life.

Missing extended family relationships in my life left me vulnerable to relationships, groups, and environments that gave me that feeling of belonging, often at the expense of personal boundaries or autonomy. I'd been searching and longing for family. I attempted to curate family in many ways. I attached myself to those who were chosen family, to volunteering my time, to ministry that was not paid, to intercession, to prophetic teams, to Sozo ministry, etc. Friends became my family, except they already had a family—one that I wasn't a part of. I now realize I was trying to get a felt sense of belonging.

Teasing out this thread in my life, I can see how becoming disconnected from my family of origin created such longing for attachments in my life. Today, I still do not have relationship with my family of origin; the last time I saw my family was at my mum's celebration of life. Other than a birthday text, I have had to face the reality that my family and I may never reconnect, and that it is not all on me to try to bridge. I share this with you as a reader because sometimes the reality is that we may not have the connections we hope for, but we can build supportive, loving, and reciprocal relationships moving forward. Not everything is for me to figure out and not everything is for you to figure out. I also have heard many stories of survivors who have gone "no contact" with their family members for the sake of their mental and emotional health. My opinion: one thread at a time. Unhook one hook and loop at a time.

In building resiliency, it was important to understand how the churches I was a part of often advocated for spiritual bypassing. If it wasn't clear already, spiritual bypassing is the tendency to use spiritual beliefs and practices to avoid facing personal, emotional, or psychological issues. This might seem contradictory, as I was part of the healing ministry in our church. As a Sozo team member, I was trained in the model and we facilitated sessions for individuals to encounter the Godhead: Father God, Jesus, and the Holy Spirit. I watched as many peoples' lives would seemingly transform. I heard the testimonies of women who said they could not get pregnant becoming pregnant. I also heard testimonies of people who suffered from years of depression suddenly finding a lifeline of hope; and no, this was not medically documented to my knowledge. Spiritual bypassing has been the root cause of many problems in my life; my trauma bond to prophecy further depleted my ability to bounce back. I carried this ache as I tried to have the faith I needed to believe, believing that speaking the word over my life or through ministry would "take care of everything" by "giving it over to God"; however, doing this would only further prolong my healing process and grief would remain unmetabolized.

One of the last times I was in church, one of the heavy hitters from Bethel Redding was visiting. I had made the trip especially to hear him speak. I remember the shock and disdain that I felt when he stood on the platform and berated anyone who was waiting for the Rapture, admonishing those who were still believing that Jesus was returning. He spoke above the people. He was there to tell you the truth, and the truth was that "Heaven was invading Earth." I listened and observed as he continued to share his testimony of how many plane trips he'd been on, in first class seats, his Air Miles status, and how many wealthy people God put in front of him. I saw arrogance, not grace. I asked myself if Jesus were here, what would He be saying? What would Jesus have to say about his platform? Who really gave them the right to speak for God? Did their life produce anything other than me, me, me—buy my books, buy my CDs? Did they have an agenda to push? Did they see a mandate rather than a person? I often heard the words "establishing the Kingdom on Earth" more than the words of Jesus. It left a bad taste in my mouth, like when someone farts beside you and you end up tasting it.

Fast forward to today, and I see that same elements at play, whether that be the next conspiracy theory or the rise of Christian nationalism. I can find myself in a tricky spot when I spend too much time in the news, especially since what I came out of is politically active both in the United States and Canada. I remind myself to stay in my wheelhouse and that taking in too much information leaves my body and brain with thoughts I'm unable to process. Having the world's information at my fingertips is not always the best. Media sensationalizes many things that can create rabbit holes. So, I focus my time and my attention on what helps, not hinders. The political realm is not my mountain to climb or my battle to fight. I purposely and thoughtfully place my vote and return to my part of the collective. There are those who are called to fight for justice, but that's not me.

With the rest of the time that I have left on this Earth, I want to focus my energy and give myself some of the opportunities I didn't have. I may not become a psychologist, but I am taking courses and receiving certifications in trauma, human development, attachment styles, and neuroscience. I may not go to school to become a teacher, but I am helping others learn the tools and skills that enable and empower them to help people heal. I may not become a hairstylist, but creativity and a holistic way of looking at life are just a part of who I am. I want to love my son and daughter well. I want to be there in life to cheer them on and support their growth. I want to be the wife and partner to Andrew that I always knew I could be—sharing and supporting each other's dreams. I want to have a harmonious relationship with my daughter-in-law, Mariah. My extended family, April, Ethan, and Richard, are family to me. I want to continue in friendships that connect me to who I have always been, who see my strengths and love me as I'm learning to roll. I want to build connections with people, groups, and communities who value humanity over ideology.

I understand what it takes to create change later in life. When I'm in conversation with those in their twenties, I see what they are talking about when they have so much information at their fingertips, a continual stream of influence that is available twenty-four seven. When I have conversations with those in their thirties, as they wonder if they have what it takes to make their dreams come true, I remind them of the opportunities they have and the time that is available to them, and then we hone in on defining their values. When

I have conversations with those in their forties, they often tell me that I'm one of the few women (who are near their mother's age) they have seen that has taken the risk to create the life they wanted rather than remain stuck. When I have conversations with those in their fifties, we often talk about what it is like to make a full pivot at this age in life, knowing that it is not uncommon. When I have conversations with those in their sixties, we often honour how far we've come, what we've come out of, reflecting that we did the work to get out, and we witness the grief that was stuffed away all those years. When I have conversations with those in their seventies and eighties, I listen. I glean from their journeys, their stories, and the wisdom that has been rewoven into their lives. When I have these conversations, I'm included in a community of those who dared, of those who dreamed, and of those who did.

I have had the privilege of hosting women's gatherings for many years. In 2018, I returned to this work by creating women's evenings, holding space for the same circle of women over the course of five years. After leaving the church, I became aware of how deeply I missed that sense of connection, the unique presence and essence that emerges when women come together. What we had in common was we were all at some stage of transition in our lives. Experiencing changes in relationships, divorces, loss of a spouse, changes in employment, we came together, shared a meal and beverage of choice, and we shared a topic. For our first gathering, I chose Brené Brown's quote on connection: "Connection is the energy that exists between people when they feel seen, heard, and valued; when they can give and receive without judgement; and when they derive sustenance and strength from the relationship."

I crafted questions and put them inside a wooden box that had a key as the top handle. Prior to dinner, each woman lifted the key and selected a folded piece of paper. After dinner, we went around the table, each sharing our question and giving our response. Then, something happened that always happens: It feels as though grace or magic entered the room, each of us felt the energy that Brené writes about. Hearts open, voices are heard, and stories begin to be told—connection in motion. If there were tears, we let them flow; if there was anger, we acknowledged that they had a right to it; and if there was grief, we solidified our boundaries and the right to feel and experience what was being experienced. When the evening ended, each of us felt lighter, freer, and bolder; it's the felt sense of that "sustenance and strength" that is quoted. The most powerful thing you can do is live as yourself.

Yes, I have come to realize that resiliency got me back on my feet, but integration gave me the ability to see more clearly and to roll more easily. Now, my life is about living from the inside out and loving it. Moving forward, I will continue to celebrate my wins; little wins add up. I have found not one, but many groups, as part of my expanding community. Dismantling and unravelling our story is one thing, understanding our story another, and making the choice to rebuild, reclaim, and recreate is work, but it's worthwhile work. Velcro Kisses may have built an attachment and bond that made it seem like they would be stuck to you forever, but that is not true; they can be undone. The funny part about Velcro Kisses is that Velcro is such a rip-off.

The third time I encountered *Educated*, I was travelling to be introduced to Andrew's mum. We walked into Chapters and there it was on the shelf. This time, Andrew had already read the book. As life would have it, the line that Andrew often said to me as encouragement was staring right at me with a picture of Tara. The book cue read, "Find out what you are capable of and then decide who you are." Fitting.

As we left the London, Ontario airport, the same airport that Andrew's parents entered Canada through in 1966, a sign hung from the ceiling that read, "Develop a good head and heart so you can lead with both; humanity needs leaders who understand our world's complex challenges and have the character to overcome them." It was advertising a university. The sign was still there the last time I visited. My mind immediately goes to meaning-making, after all, it's had years of practice. I tend to be an internal processor. I took a picture of the poster because it resonated with me in some way, but I didn't have time to stop and think. I've looked at that snapshot many times over the last eight years, and I've come to adopt that stance in life. I do believe that we need more heart-centred and mind-balanced people and systems —systems that are not based on full immersion with intense and all-or-nothing teachings.

Now every time I return to the past, whether in memory or on the page, I meet a different version of myself. Each one carries a piece of the woman I was becoming all along. For years, I mistook silence for strength and enmeshment for safety. But now, I understand that true freedom isn't found in forgetting, it's found in remembering without fear. And true healing isn't about erasing who I was but reclaiming the parts I gave away and releasing what no longer serves me. Writing has become a doorway, and with each word, I reclaim my story—not to prove anything, but to stand inside it, finally home.

The girl you once were is still part of me, and the woman you are becoming will carry her forward.

—Future Susan

Acknowledgements

Writing this book has been a journey and one I could not have completed alone. This book is both a reflection of where I've been and a sign of what's possible, and it's about learning to appreciate the space in between.

To those who were part of my life during seasons marked by both connection and loss—family, chosen family, and community—thank you. Some relationships were shaped by love and support, while others brought heartache and loss. Like the seasons, relationships change, and with them, we grow. Writing this book became my way to face my wounds, to grieve what was lost, and to do the work of healing. Through this process, I've found strength, clarity, and a deeper understanding of what it means to heal deeply. In that healing, I have reclaimed my voice—finding the courage to speak my truth, let go, and move forward. Each chapter helped prepare me for the chapter that followed, even up to this present moment.

To those who stayed close when I lost my footing, thank you. Your presence reminded me that falling isn't failure; it's part of becoming. Your kindness gave me the room I needed to catch my breath. Your encouragement gave me the strength to learn to roll, rise again, find my balance, and move forward, one brave step at a time. I'm deeply grateful to the Knight family for the way you opened your hearts and your home to my family.

To those I brought into this world, Benjamin and Abigail, I will never be able to express my thanks for your belief in me; that even at my age, change is possible. Your support and excitement helped me give myself the permission I needed to move forward.

To Debra and Gary, you carry yourselves with such kindness, integrity, and generosity. Being on the receiving end of that has been profoundly meaningful. To Susan, thank you for being my cheerleader in this life. Each of you have continued to believe in me and reminded me that growth doesn't always come in grand gestures, but in giving oneself the permission to try and try again. Thank you for celebrating the small wins with me as I found my footing, balance, and rhythm again. I am grateful for our continued connection in life's journey.

To Andrew, your love and support has been a soft place to land. Oopsie-daisy twice over. In all my falls, you reminded me I was never alone. Now I really get what it means to have a wingman. You walk your talk. Thank you for nurturing my dreams and cheering me on through this writing process, from the cups of tea to the way you've encouraged me to fully step into this journey—thank you.

To the voices and stories that met me in unexpected ways, you helped me see that healing isn't always a straight line. There are often twists and turns, but it's in learning and giving yourself permission to begin again—all sprinkled with wonder and magic—that we find our true selves.

To the quiet strength that carried me when I felt too tired to keep going—thank you.

And to you, dear reader, if you find yourself somewhere in the in-between, know this: Falling doesn't mean you've failed. Rolling is part of the rhythm. And balance, however it finds you, can be both gentle and powerful. Keep going. There's more ahead than you can yet imagine.

With love,
Susan

References

American Psychiatric Association. *Diagnostic and Statistical Manual of Mental Disorders: DSM-5.* 5th ed. Arlington, VA: American Psychiatric Publishing, 2013.

Bible Gateway. 2025. *New King James Version Bible.* Accessed October 16, 2025. https://www.biblegateway.com/versions/New-King-James-Version-NKJV-Bible/

Bickel, Jim. "History Is His Story." Sermon, Bethel Baptist Fellowship, May 15, 2022. Accessed October 16, 2025. https://bethelbaptistfellowship.org/messages/history-is-his-story/.

Brown, Brené. *Rising Strong: How the Ability to Reset Transforms the Way We Live, Love, Parent, and Lead.* Paperback edition. New York: Random House, 2017. ISBN 978-0-8129-8580-1.

Eskridge, Larry. *God's Forever Family: The Jesus People Movement in America.* Oxford: Oxford University Press, 2013.

Gordon T. Kraft-Todd, David G. Rand, Practice what you preach: Credibility-enhancing displays and the growth of open science, Organizational Behavior and Human

Decision Processes, Volume 164, 2021, Pages 1–10, ISSN
0749-5978, https://doi.org/10.1016/j.obhdp.2020.10.009.

Hassan, Steven. *Combating Cult Mind Control: The #1
Best-Selling Guide to Protection, Rescue, and Recovery
from Destructive Cults*. Paperback edition. Newton, MA:
Freedom of Mind Press, March 27, 2015.
ISBN 978-0-967068-82-4

Heller, Diane Poole. The Power of Attachment: *How to
Create Deep and Lasting Intimate Relationships.* North Star
Press, 2019.

*How To BRAINWASH Yourself For Success & Destroy
NEGATIVE THOUGHTS!* | Dr. Joe Dispenza. YouTube
video, June 12, 2018. https://www.youtube.com/
watch?v=La9oLLoI5Rc&t.

Hunter, John. *Manufacturing Mania: The Dopamine
Hypothesis of Religious Experience*. Independently published,
2024.

Jakes, T. D. *Woman, Thou Art Loosed!: Healing the Wounds of
the Past*. Destiny Image, 2016.

Jones, Martyn Wendell. "Inside the Popular,
Controversial Bethel Church." *Christianity
Today*, May 2016. Accessed October 16, 2025.
https://www.christianitytoday.com/2016/04/
cover-story-inside-popular-controversial-bethel-church/.

Lalich, Janja. *Take Back Your Life: Recovering from Cults & Abusive Relationships*. 3rd ed., Lalich Center on Cults & Coercion, 2023.

Maxwell, John C. *Failing Forward: Turning Mistakes into Stepping Stones for Success*. Nashville: Thomas Nelson Publishers, 2000.

Peterson, Anne L. *Is This a Cult? Confronting the Line Between Transformation and Exploitation*. Independently published, 2024.

Shaw, Daniel. *TN Clinical Utility*. January 2025. PDF. DanielShawLCSW.com. Accessed October 16, 2025. https://danielshawlcsw.com/wp-content/uploads/2025/01/TN-Clinical-Utility.pdf.

Schrader, Maria, dir. *She Said*. Universal Pictures, 2022.

The Family Systems Institute. "Definitions from Bowen Theory." The FSI. Accessed October 16, 2025. https://www.thefsi.com.au/definitions-from-bowen-theory/.

"Toronto Blessing," *Encyclopedia.com*, updated June 27, 2018. Accessed October 16, 2025. https://www.encyclopedia.com/philosophy-and-religion/christianity/christianity-general/toronto-blessing

Upton, Jason. *Freedom Reigns*. Key of David Ministries, 2000. MP3.

About the Author

Susan Stirling has worn many hats over the years: daughter, sister, wife, and mother. She has been a business partner, coach, spiritual worker, and teammate—sometimes all of them in the same week. She has walked alongside individuals finding their footing, couples navigating change, businesses chasing big dreams, and non-profits working to make a difference. Each connection has left its mark, shaping not just the work she did, but the person she has become. If there's one thing she's learned—it's that the journey changes you. Today, she works with individuals untangling their own complex histories—especially those navigating patterned self-abandonment, undue influence, or religious and spiritual trauma. With a trauma-sensitive lens, as well as being a certified coach based on the neuroscience of human development, Susan helps others discover the power of small steps, safe connections, and living from the inside out.